Students and Dyslexia:

Growing up with a Specific Learning Difficulty

Students and Dyslexia:

Growing up with a Specific Learning Difficulty

by
Barbara Riddick,
Education Department, University of Newcastle
Marion Farmer,
Psychology Department, University of Northumbria
and
Christopher Sterling,
Psychology Department, University of Northumbria

Whurr Publishers Ltd
London

©1997 Whurr Publishers Ltd

First published 1997
Whurr Publishers Ltd
19B Compton Terrace,
London N1 2UN,
England

Reprinted 2003

British Library Cataloguing in Publication Data
A catalogue record for this book is available from the British Library.

ISBN 1 86156 041 9

Printed and bound in the UK by Athenaeum Press Ltd, Gateshead, Tyne and Wear

Contents

Preface

As part of a wider research study on dyslexia it was decided to include in-depth interviews with university students. On listening to these accounts, we felt that they provided such a compelling testament to the experiences of growing up with dyslexia that we ought to publish the interviews in a form that left them to speak largely for themselves. As students volunteered for this study we cannot be sure how representative they are of students with dyslexia in general, but what was striking was the wide range of social and economic backgrounds of the students. They also varied considerably in age and life development, ranging from those still in their teens who had just left home to middle-aged mature students with children of their own. Although this presented problems for our more empirical research, we felt it provided a rich and diverse picture of students with dyslexia. We were very fortunate to have an enthusiastic young research assistant, Steven Morgan, who was dyslexic himself, to carry out the interviews and we feel sure that his insight and understanding enabled him to develop a good rapport with the interviewees. In the *Narrative Study of Lives*, Josselson and Lieblich (1993) talk about 'trying to get to the core of people's lived experience' and argue that conventional psychology often misses out on this more holistic perspective. This is what we hope these interviews provide.

A second reason for publishing this book is that higher education in the UK has recently undergone considerable change, especially in the overall increase in student numbers and the greater number of mature students and students with non-traditional academic backgrounds. We cannot be sure, but our impression was that several of our mature students had been delayed in their entry to university largely because of their dyslexia. In addition, it appears that the increased understanding and identification of dyslexia has led to a huge increase in the number of students being recognised as dyslexic. All this raises important questions about how a diverse range of students with dyslexia can best be identified and supported at both college and university. We hope these accounts may be of help to other students or prospective students with dyslexia, and also to the people teaching them.

Another point is that all the students gave vivid and detailed accounts of their time at school and several of them commented that university was easy in comparison with the struggles they had encountered at school. Because the students were able to reflect on their own experiences over time in coping with the difficulties surrounding their dyslexia they were able to provide a strong developmental perspective. In illustrating how they survived, or in some cases were supported by, school, we felt that there was much of relevance and interest to children with dyslexia and their families and to teachers in both primary and secondary schools.

Chapter 1 introduces the study and briefly reviews some of the present definitions of dyslexia, and considers some of the key points to emerge from research and clinical experience with both children and adults. Chapter 2 outlines the present study and the methodology that was used. Chapters 3 to 11 present the accounts of individual students and look at how these relate to some of the wider theoretical and practical issues surrounding dyslexia. Chapter 12 concludes by drawing together some of the main issues that have been raised and looks at how these can be tackled.

Finally, although there is still debate in the UK about the term 'dyslexia', with some educationalists preferring the term 'specific learning difficulties', dyslexia was the term used throughout the research project. In recruiting students we found that dyslexia was the term that students used both to identify and to understand their own difficulties. Although this may be an are for further debate, we would argue that if we are to understand people's subjective experiences we have to respect and understand the way that they choose to define themselves.

Acknowledgements

Firstly, we would like to thank all the students who took part in the study, and especially the students with dyslexia who participated in the in-depth interviews. It is their courage and willingness to talk about their personal experiences of dyslexia that have made this book possible.

Secondly, we would like to acknowledge the vital contribution of our research assistant Steven Morgan in collecting much of the data.

Finally, we would like to thank Margaret Snowling for her constructive comments on the final draft of the book.

Chapter 1
Introduction

Although it may be argued that students with dyslexia are not representative of the wider population of individuals with dyslexia, they nevertheless form an interesting and informative group to study. At a common-sense level they appear to be a relatively successful group of individuals with dyslexia who, despite their literacy difficulties, have done sufficiently well in the education system to obtain a place at university. This immediately raises a number of questions about how they have managed to succeed and what environmental and personal variables appear to be critical in this process. It also raises questions about how they are performing relative to other students, and how they perceive and cope with the specific difficulties that they have. This in turn raises another set of questions about the nature of their specific difficulties and the degree of difference both in the nature and in the severity of difficulties between individual students who have been identified as having dyslexia.

Fundamental Difficulties

In order to answer some of the above questions it is helpful to look at some of the general literature on dyslexia and briefly to review some of the relevant research. Because dyslexia was first characterised as a reading and writing difficulty, until recently much of the focus was on this aspect, especially in educational settings. Dyslexia was often defined as an unexpected difficulty in learning to read and write in someone of average or above-average intelligence. Reading and writing (including spelling) can be seen as behaviours or outcomes of underlying thinking or cognitive processes, and more recent researchers have argued that to understand dyslexia it is necessary to understand where the difficulties might be in these underlying processes. Although this is still an active area for research and debate, at a very general level it is agreed that dyslexia probably involves some difficulty in phonological processing, in other words, with learning about various aspects of the sound system underpinning language.

Allied to these difficulties are impairments in auditory short-term or working memory. A 'phoneme' is the term used by linguists to describe the smallest element of sound that can distinguish one word from another. The words 'cat' and 'cut' are distinguished by their middle phonemes, but phonemes do not always correspond to single letters, and some sounds are represented by a combination of letters such as 'ch' or 'th'. The range of problems that individuals with dyslexia have with these sound-based aspects of language fall under the general title of phonological processing difficulties, and there is now a wide body of research looking at various aspects of these. Some of the most influential research in this area has been on the development of phonological awareness in young children (Bradley and Bryant, 1985). The significant point is that research with children as young as 3 and 4 years old has found that those children who have difficulty in identifying aspects of the sound system such as words that rhyme are more likely to have difficulty in learning to read. At the other end of the spectrum it has also been found that adults with dyslexia are poorer than average on a number of phonological tasks (Bruck, 1992). This suggests that there are persistent cognitive impairments underlying dyslexia.

An example of a task used to look at one aspect of phonological processing is the non-word reading task (Snowling, 1980). This involves reading a list of plausibly spelt words such as 'wub' or 'grimsket', which do not actually exist in the English language. In the majority of studies, individuals with dyslexia have as a group performed poorly on this task compared with non-dyslexic individuals. The assumption is that because these words are not familiar to them they cannot read them by using their visual memory and are forced into using their weaker phonological skills. There has been a large amount of research in this area, which it is not possible to review here, but, for interested readers, good summaries are provided by Ellis (1993) and Hulme and Snowling (1994). One of the key questions at present is how far early identification and intervention can ameliorate these impairments and how far it is a question of teaching or enabling individuals to find strategies that help them to compensate for or avoid their impairments.

Although there has been considerable interest in phonological impairments, a number of researchers have suggested that there may also be other impairments underlying the performance of all or some individuals with dyslexia. For example, Fawcett and Nicolson (1994) have argued that there may be more fundamental processing difficulties that give rise to a number of impairments in other areas such as fine motor skills in addition to phonological impairments. This would help explain the high proportion of children with dyslexia who also have problems with tasks such as handwriting and tying shoe laces. In this case they argue that the basic impairment is in the ability to automatise various skills. The advantage of carrying out a process automatically is that it allows it to be done rapidly and with little demand on a person's overall processing capacity, and it is also carried out unconsciously and is therefore not disrupted by other competing activities. Where a skill is not automatic more processing capacity is needed and the task is experienced as more effortful. Recent research on inexperienced drivers has demonstrated that their basic problem is one of information-processing overload, whereas experienced drivers carry out many of the physical tasks of driving automatically and therefore have more processing capacity available for monitoring road conditions. Fawcett and Nicolson (1992) found that dyslexic children did as well as non-dyslexic children on a series of balancing tasks such as walking along a beam, but when they were required at the same time to carry out another task, such as counting backwards, the dyslexic children performed far worse than they had before on the balancing task and far worse than the non-dyslexic children, whose performance showed no deterioration. Evidence like this was taken to indicate that dyslexic children can consciously compensate by putting more effort into a task, but when they are required to carry out two competing tasks they are either prevented from compensating or are overloaded so that their performance suffers. Although it is speculative at the moment, Fawcett and Nicolson are currently investigating the proposal that the cerebellum is centrally involved in these automatisation difficulties. Whatever the underlying cause of these proposed difficulties it is not difficult to imagine the problems they will pose with a complex skill such as reading, and it is interesting to note that some adults with dyslexia still describe reading as an effortful and frustrating task. In a series of studies, Yapp and van der Leij (1994) found that dyslexics needed extra time in order to use compensatory strategies on a reading task, and commented that 'compensation is an effortful, time consuming process'. In a similar way, several of the dyslexic students in our study made comments emphasising the extra time and effort they had to put into reading. June, for example, said 'I have to take twice as long to do my reading'.

Another area in which there is renewed interest is that of possible visual processing difficulties. Lovegrove (1994) in Australia and Stein (1994) in the UK have carried out extensive research into these deficits, and both have concluded that there may be problems with the transient visual system. Lovegrove outlines the two major visual subsystems as the transient system that processes rapidly moving information and the sustained system that processes slow-moving information. On the basis of his research, Lovegrove concludes that dyslexics do not show any impairment in the sustained system but they do show impairments in the transient system. In reading, the transient system is important for integrating information and the two systems have to be well co-ordinated for a string of words to be clearly perceived. If the transient system is not performing effectively it will interfere with the process of reading. Stein has suggested that this deficit in the transient system may lead to poor eye movement control and poor ability to co-ordinate the two eyes in order to have stable binocular vision. Three out of the sixteen dyslexic students interviewed in our study reported the kind of visual experiences that would suggest this kind of unstable visual control. Andy, for example, found that words moved around the page and had been forced to try and develop strategies to deal with this. 'When I'm approached with closely written stuff I like to put a card underneath to block out the words underneath so that my eyes aren't strained and then I'll point to the words, but the more tired I get the more difficult it is'. Critics (Bishop, 1989; Pumfrey and Reason, 1991) have argued that it is in fact the language-based problems in processing the text that lead to the eye movement problems, rather than the eye movement problems leading to the reading problems. Stein has countered these arguments by pointing out that intervention (covering 1 eye for 6 months) which gave some children stable binocular control also led to an improvement in their reading age. This is still contentious and more research is needed. Stein acknowledges that one of the difficulties with accepting that visual problems have anything to do with dyslexia has been the overwhelming evidence for a phonological (sound) basis to dyslexia. He suggests that rather than seeing these two theories as in opposition it is possible to look at the evidence for both visual and phonological deficits coexisting and emerging from one underlying source. Several researchers (Galaburda, 1985; Lovegrove, 1991; Livingstone et al., 1991; Stein, 1994) have suggested that these underlying deficits are in the magnocellular system of the central nervous system, which is involved in rapid signal processing in all the different senses.

The overall message seems to be that although considerable progress has been made in identifying the cognitive impairments underlying dyslexia, it is important to keep an open mind and accept that there may be several underlying deficits, rather than one, that result in an individual's having literacy difficulties. Allied to this there may be subtypes within dyslexia that have rather different cognitive strengths and weaknesses, and each type in turn may vary in severity. Opinion is divided as to whether dyslexia should be seen as a qualitatively different disorder or simply the bottom end of the continuum between individuals with good or poor literacy skills. Whichever approach is taken, it is clear there is a group of individuals who have quite specific impairments in reading, writing and spelling at odds with their general reasoning or thinking skills. Estimations as to the size of this group vary but several authorities suggest that about 4% of the population have severe dyslexia and that a further 6% have mild to moderate difficulties (Miles and Miles, 1990; Peer, 1994).

Long-term Outcomes

It is only quite recently that dyslexia or specific learning difficulties have been widely acknowledged and researched. Much of this research has focused on younger children and the specific difficulties of learning to read. Although clinical accounts have long pointed to difficulties in older children and adults, there is still relatively little research in this area and the long-term nature of the impairments underlying dyslexia are only just beginning to be fully appreciated. The majority of individuals with dyslexia do eventually learn to read, but large numbers of them continue to have considerable difficulties with spelling, aspects of grammar such as word endings and punctuation, and many report that writing in particular takes them considerably longer than non-dyslexic individuals. Beaton, McDougall and Singleton (1997) provide a useful overview of some of the recent research in this area. One of the key points to emerge is that on a whole range of tasks the majority of dyslexic students and adults showed phonological processing difficulties (Gottardo, Siegal and Stanovich, 1997; Snowling et al., 1997). Despite this, there did appear to be a smaller subgroup of individuals with dyslexia who in some studies (Hanley, 1997; Rack, 1997) did not display phonological processing difficulties, again emphasising the need to keep an open mind and not rely on phonological difficulties as the sole indicator of dyslexia. Shaywitz (1996) reports that in the Connecticut Longitudinal Study, which followed 445 randomly selected kindergarten children through to the age of 19 years, those children who were initially identified as having dyslexia showed evidence of specific phonological impairments linked to poor reading in their teens. Evidence is thus mounting that the specific impairments underlying dyslexia do persist in adulthood and that, despite compensatory strategies, they do impair the performance of dyslexic students on specific aspects of literacy tasks.

Because dyslexia has been researched from an educational perspective it is those literacy skills closely linked to educational achievement that have been most extensively researched. An area that has been far less researched is the impact of underlying cognitive impairments, such as poor short-term memory, on everyday living. Most of what is known at present comes from clinical accounts.

Secondary Difficulties

In a similar vein, although clinical and personal accounts have long pointed to the emotional and social distress that individuals with dyslexia can experience, there has been relatively little systematic research into this area. What is clear is that there are a number of possible secondary consequences to growing up with dyslexia such as low self-esteem, anxiety and poor motivation at school. What is also clear is that the way that the environment responds to the individual plays a large part in their overall well-being and response to their difficulties, although other factors such as the severity of the difficulties and the personality of the individual may be critical as well. McLoughlin, Fitzgibbon and Young (1994) comment that although adults with dyslexia can be successful, 'It is however common for dyslexic adults to be faced with emotional, psychological and social difficulties, which make success harder to achieve'.

One of the major differences in considering adults and children with dyslexia is that the discrepancy between reading and spelling ages and children's actual (chronological) age, which is one of the keystones of assessment in childhood, is not appropriate for adults. More sensitive forms of reading, writing and spelling tests are needed for adults, which focus on speed as well as accuracy and are as close to the complex sort of reading and writing tasks demanded in real-world situations. In conjunction with this, tasks that look at the possible difficulties in underlying processes are helpful in assessing difficulties in both adults and children. Speece (1987) found that 76% of adults with learning disabilities showed deficits in their processing speed. McLoughlin, Fitzgibbon and Young (1994) argue that it is more productive to characterise dyslexia in adulthood as a problem with short-term or working memory than simply as a literacy problem. Riddick (1995) has similarly argued that there needs to be a better appreciation of the cognitive deficits underlying dyslexia in order for there to be a wider understanding of the range of tasks that may be affected.

Another issue that arises when considering an individual's performance is the degree to which difficulties are primary or secondary in nature. Someone who experienced considerable difficulty with consequent embarrassment and humiliation when asked to read out loud as a young child may experience these same feelings of anxiety and humiliation as an adult, despite the fact that if they were not so anxious they could perform the task reasonably well. At present there are few longitudinal studies that have followed children with dyslexia into adulthood, so it is often unclear when looking at the performance of adults how far these are a reflection of their current cognitive abilities and how far they are influenced by their feelings about their past experiences.

Personal Well-being

In reviewing evidence on the long-term well-being of poor readers, Maughan (1994) concludes that as adults there is little evidence of serious mental health problems, but there may be an increased risk of anxiety and depressed mood. In fact, longitudinal studies by Bruck (1985) in Canada and by Spreen (1987) in London suggest that there are much higher rates of disturbance during the school years and that these drop considerably once such children have left school. The inference we can draw from this is that once individuals have left the high and public literacy demands of the school environment they fare much better in terms of personal well-being. This raises interesting questions about the well-being of university students with dyslexia. As they have chosen to enter an environment that demands high literacy skills, do they feel under the same pressures as at school or are these a self-selected group of individuals who have found successful ways of coping with their literacy problems?

Areas of Research

In looking at research specifically on students with dyslexia, we can identify a number of issues and areas. Research can focus on the specific literacy and cognitive impairments, on the emotional and social well-being, and on the coping strategies and long-term outcomes for such students. Research can also look at what ideally should happen in terms of identification and support, and also evaluate current practice and the feasibility and efficacy of various forms of assessment and intervention.

Degrees of Impairment

An important area for future research is to distinguish between students with different degrees of impairments, and consider the levels of support appropriate to these different degrees. Although at a clinical level we know individuals vary in the severity and nature of their problems, attempts to quantify these differences are at an early stage. In the case of hearing and visual impairments, we are all familiar with the idea that people can vary considerably in the nature and severity of their impairments, and someone with a visual impairment could range from an individual who is slightly short-sighted to someone who has no light-dark vision and is classified as totally blind. Perhaps because dyslexia is a 'hidden' disability with no obvious physical markers the range in severity is harder to quantify and has received less attention than it deserves. Critics of the term would also argue that a label like 'dyslexia' implies a one-off entity, something that you either have or do not have and that is not in itself conducive to the concept of a continuum, which is why they would prefer a term like 'specific learning difficulties', which it is easier to conceive of individuals having to different degrees. It also underlines the importance of having appropriate and sufficiently sensitive norm-referenced tests that compare an individual with dyslexia with both the non-dyslexic population and others with dyslexia.

National Working Party on Dyslexia in Higher Education

At present, the National Working Party on Dyslexia in Higher Education is considering the needs of dyslexic students in the UK and has collected information from a wide variety of sources, including leading academics, practitioners and clinicians in the field. An important part of their report focuses on issues of assessment and appropriate levels of support. Any assessment of an individual student's needs also has to take into account the literacy demands of the course that the student is following. A degree in Fine Art or in Maths, for example, will usually place fewer literacy demands on the student than a degree in Law or Education, although individual courses even within a subject area can vary considerably in the literacy demands that they make. Whether the course is assessed by exams or assignments or some proportion of each may also be important, as many students with dyslexia feel that they do worse under timed conditions.

US Research

Much of what research there is on students with dyslexia comes from the USA. The difficulty in interpreting these data is that most focus on a somewhat wider group of students, who fall under the umbrella title of 'learning disabled'. On the other hand, most of the students who in the UK would be identified as having dyslexia or specific learning difficulties would seem to fall under this label, so although the data need to be used with caution, they are of value.

Research on Literacy Difficulties

Research into literacy difficulties has looked primarily at reading, spelling and writing problems. Each of these areas in turn has been broken down into various components; so, for example, reading problems include problems related to the speed and accuracy of reading materials of different levels of difficulty and familiarity and the time needed to extract meaning from what is read. Evidence from the general adult population of individuals with dyslexia indicates that for a significant proportion some degree of reading problems do persist (Balow and Bloomquist, 1965; Hardy, 1968). Studies by Brown, Bennett and Hanna (1981), Hill (1984) and Runyan (1991) have demonstrated that dyslexic subjects fare as well as non-dyslexic subjects on the Nelson-Denny Reading Test under untimed conditions, but fare worse under timed conditions. Many, but not all, dyslexic students report that reading takes them longer and that they often have to reread things several times to extract the meaning.

Spelling has been identified as one of the most persistent and intractable difficulties displayed by individuals with dyslexia. Klein (1993) reports spelling as the most frequently mentioned difficulty by students with dyslexia. Deno, Marston and Mirkin (1982) report that students with learning disabilities (LDs) make two to four times the number of spelling errors made by non-learning-disabled students in their written work. Bryson and Siegal (1986) and MacArthur and Graham (1987) both estimate that learning-disabled students misspell 10–20 % of the words that they write. Graham (1990) has suggested that one of the knock-on effects of this is that if a student has to stop and think how to spell a word this may disrupt their train of thought and therefore the quality and fluency of their written expression. Mosely (1989) has demonstrated that children often avoid words that they cannot spell, and personal accounts verify that many adults also use this strategy. The difficulty with this strategy is that students may produce work that appears less sophisticated in content and, particularly if compounded by poor punctuation and grammar as well as poor handwriting, it is in danger of creating a negative impression irrespective of the ideas embodied within it. Spellcheckers have been suggested as an easy way for students with dyslexia to correct their spelling mistakes. Although research shows that spellcheckers do enable students to pick up a percentage of their spelling mistakes, it also indicates that the more severe and frequent the mistakes are the less likely they are to be correctly rectified. An obvious difficulty is that the more idiosyncratic someone's spelling is the less likely it is that the spellchecker will able to suggest the correct spelling. An additional difficulty is that where the correct spelling is one of several options provided, those individuals with poor spelling are the least able to pick out the correct one. MacArthur et al. (1996) found in a series of studies on the use of spellcheckers by learning-disabled students that under 40% of their spelling mistakes were successfully corrected using a spellchecker. Although spelling errors are often seen as the characteristic feature of the written work of students with dyslexia, for many of them a number of language-based errors and poor punctuation are just as prevalent. Common language-based difficulties are unintentionally omitting words such as pronouns and leaving the endings off of words. It is often suggested to students with dyslexia that they should proofread their work, the assumption being that this would enable them to correct the majority of their errors. In reality, this is a very difficult task, as individuals tend to read what they think is there rather than exactly what is there, so it is easy, for example, not to notice that a word is missing. On top of this, spelling errors often are not picked up because the person assumes that the way they have spelt a word in the first place is the correct way. Systematic research on proofread-ing and the nature and frequency of the errors that are and are not picked up is needed, as much of what is known at present is impres-sionistic in nature.

An area of specific importance to students is note-taking skills, and several studies (Kiewra and Fletcher, 1984; Baker and Lombardi,

1985; Einstein, Morris and Smith, 1985) have reported that there is a direct link between the amount of information recorded in students' notes and their performance in exams. It has been reported that students with learning disabilities/dyslexia claim to have difficulties with note-taking for a variety of reasons. One difficulty with self-report studies is that it is not known in reality how such students perform compared with ordinary students. A study by Hughes and Suritsky (1994) set out to address this specific question by comparing the note-taking skills of thirty learning-disabled and thirty non-learning-disabled students; they found that on all the performance indicators selected the learning-disabled students as a group did significantly worse. It was found that one of the major difficulties experienced by the learning-disabled students was that they were poorer at picking out what the significant pieces of information to record were. Note-taking is a complex skill and other factors such as slow handwriting and less use of abbreviations are also implicated; more research is needed to look at the variety of factors involved.

A difficulty frequently mentioned by students with dyslexia is that writing tasks take them longer to do and that they therefore have to spend longer than other students on completing assignments. There is a paucity of evidence on writing speeds in adults, but Hedderly (1996) suggests that 20 words per minute is about average for the adult population. The difficulty with assessing writing speed is that factors such as motivation and the subject being written about have an influence on writing speed, so that it is difficult to separate out the thinking and planning time from the mechanics of writing time. Some but not all individuals with dyslexia have poor handwriting, and Miles (1983), on the basis of a large number of case studies, comments on the atrocious handwriting of many individuals with dyslexia. Although visual-perceptual difficulties could be implicated in poor handwriting, there is mounting evidence that children with dyslexia display difficulties across a range of motor tasks (Haslum, 1989; Fawcett and Nicolson, 1994). Other researchers, such as Rudel (1985), have demonstrated that children with dyslexia do not have problems with the perceptual aspect of the task and that the difficulty appears to be one of fine motor co-ordination. Whatever underlies poor handwriting, it does lead to problems of illegibility, slow speed and extra effort, with some individuals even having problems in reading their own writing. These problems are not exclusive to individuals with dyslexia but at a clinical level they are commonly reported, and more research on the frequency and nature of these difficulties would be welcome.

Social and Emotional Consequences

Given the persistence of underlying processing deficits and the attendant range of literacy difficulties that many students with dyslexia are
still encountering, an important question is, how do they cope with
these difficulties and what sort of impact do these have on their self-
perception and general well-being? Evidence already exists that children with dyslexia or poor reading tend to have low self-esteem, so an
initial question is, do students with dyslexia tend to have lower than
average self-esteem? Several studies of learning-disabled students
have reported low self-esteem, lack of confidence, frustration and
insecurity. The difficulty is that these studies were often poorly
controlled with poor sampling, measures and comparison groups,
but, combined with the clinical evidence, there is a strong suspicion
that students with dyslexia are at greater risk of low self-esteem.
Although it is still more tentative, there is also some suggestion that
students with learning disabilities are at greater risk of social difficulties. What is not clear is whether this is linked in some way to their
underlying processing difficulties or is entirely a secondary outcome
of their reaction to their specific literacy difficulties (Kavale and
Forness, 1996). Many would agree with Price, Johnson and Evelo
(1994) that there has been insufficient attention paid to the social and
emotional consequences of learning disabilities, and that too often
support services have focused primarily on the literacy problems.

Coping Strategies

In recent times both clinicians and researchers have suggested that
self-awareness and self-advocacy are important in helping individuals to make the best of living with their specific difficulties (Phillips,
1990; McLoughlin, Fitzgibbon and Young, 1994; Ruffian, Herzog
and Wersham-Gershon, 1994). McLoughlin, Fitzgibbon and Young
argue that self-awareness, in terms of individuals understanding
their strengths and weaknesses, is essential if they are to develop
effective compensatory strategies. They have listed four stages in the
development of awareness and compensatory strategies, with stage 4
seen as the most effective:

Stage 1.   No awareness – no compensatory strategies
Stage 2.   Awareness – no compensatory strategies developed.
Stage 3.   Awareness – unconscious compensatory strategies
                developed.

Stage 4.   Awareness – conscious compensatory strategies
                  developed.

Studies in the USA have documented the coping strategies learning-disabled students have used. Goldberg (1983) found that 57 such students at a competitive university reported that they had to put more time and effort into their work than other students and that many of them sought help from the university support services. Cowen (1988) studied 28 learning-disabled students. She found correlations between subjects' self-reports of their literacy difficulties and their performance on standardised reading, spelling and writing tests of between 92 and 100%, indicating that they had a realistic picture of their own difficulties. This may have been partly because 76% had previously attended colleges with specialist awareness and support services. Despite the high level of awareness, 76% of the students still reported difficulties with their grammar, spelling and punctuation, 72% reported difficulties with taking adequate notes, and 76% reported difficulties with reading tests or writing exam answers. In writing tasks, although subjects reported using a variety of coping strategies, such as looking words up in dictionaries, they felt that none of these strategies was entirely successful and 54% relied on others to proofread their work. What was significant was that students were not using such coping strategies as taping lectures, applying for extra time in exams, or using word processors or taped books to any great extent. Although, at an impressionistic level, it is probable that UK students have made increasing use of these strategies, the fundamental point remains that students should be encouraged to use strategies that help them to compensate or bypass their difficulties as well as being given help to improve their skills.

Successful Adults

Another approach tried in the USA in particular has been to attempt to identify those factors that seem most closely associated with successful adults with learning disabilities. Scott, Scherman and Phillips (1992) interviewed a number of successful adults with dyslexia, and found that all of them had a strong sense of purpose and had developed a sense of self-worth, partly through hobbies or personal interests. When asked what had made them successful, they highlighted 'persistence, hard work and their internal personal drive'. Gerber, Ginsberg and Reiff (1992) studied 46 individuals with learning disabilities who had been highly successful in employment

terms, and an additional 25 who had been moderately successful.
They found that 89% of these individuals had degrees and that over
50% of the highly successful group had doctorates. As in other studies, the adults stressed that they often had to work harder than others
and that persistence and determination were essential. A key over-
arching theme that was identified by these researchers was that
successful adults take control of their lives and work towards clearly
identified and achievable goals. Despite being successful, many of
these adults still talked about their past failure at school and the irrel-
evance of school to their present success. Gerber, Reiff and Ginsberg
(1996) have argued that what many successful adults do is to reframe
their experiences of learning disability in a more positive and
productive manner. Most of the studies on successful adults have
been retrospective in nature and have asked adults to talk about their
past experiences and to describe what makes them successful at
present. This gives a good picture of what a successful adult looks
like, but does not really explain why these individuals as opposed to
others should have the qualities that lead to success. Greenbaum,
Graham and Scales (1996) note that when the majority of studies on
adults with learning disabilities are considered the results are worry-
ing, with a disproportionate number of individuals unemployed or in
menial, low-paid jobs. Perhaps not surprisingly, level of education
has been identified as a critical factor in success, with people of the
same degree of disability who stay on at school doing better than
those that leave school (Edgar, 1987; Zigmond and Thorton, 1985).
Several studies have identified social class, IQ and severity of disability as the critical factors that influence the level of both educational
and occupational success for individuals with learning disabilities
(Vogel, Hruby and Alderman, 1993; Bruck, 1987; Hartzell and
Compton, 1984). Similarly, Greenbaum, Graham and Scales (1996)
found that the 49 learning-disabled adults that they interviewed had
a higher than average IQ for the college they were attending, a
higher socio-economic background level, and mild to moderate
rather than severe learning disabilities. In this and many other studies participants also emphasised that the support of their family,
especially while they were at school, was of critical importance.
Overall, it seems important to take account of social, cognitive and
personal factors and the interaction between them in trying to get as
full a picture as possible as to what enables adults with dyslexia to feel
that they have done themselves justice.

Labelling

There has been an ongoing debate about the possible consequences of giving people a specific label such as dyslexia. In the 1960s and 1970s strong arguments were put forward for the negative consequences of labelling. It was argued that labelling led to stigmatisation, discrimination, negative stereotyping and emphasised the disability rather than the person. These arguments had a profound influence on educational policy and practice, and may help account for some of the reluctance to use a term such as 'dyslexia'. But more recent examination of this issue suggests that the arguments are more complex and that both positive and negative outcomes can accompany the use of labels. Riddick (1995, 1996) argues that the nature, purpose and context in which a label is applied has to be taken into account. She found that the children she interviewed made a clear distinction between the private and public usage of the label 'dyslexia'. At a private level nearly all the children in the sample thought that the label helped them to understand their difficulties and feel more positive about themselves, whereas half of them did not find the label helpful at a public level, mainly because of fear of teasing or ridicule by other children. The children's parents also stressed the importance of having a label in terms of both understanding and being able to develop positive coping strategies. Both the children and the parents argued that in many cases they had already been informally labelled as 'thick' or 'lazy' by some children and teachers, and the label 'dyslexia' could at least be used to counter these false assumptions.

In the USA, Barga (1996) also notes that the eight learning-disabled students that she interviewed also distinguished between the positive and negative aspects of labelling, and that they also found labelling helpful at a private level but more mixed at a public level, where, on the positive side, it could lead to access to more resources and better understanding but, on the negative side, it could lead to gate-keeping (i.e. being advised not to take certain courses) and stigmatisation. It has to be pointed out that only two out of the eight students she interviewed had the specific label 'dyslexia' in addition to the more general label of 'learning disabilities', and this may therefore have influenced the sort of outcomes that were reported. Practitioners in the UK such as McLoughlin, Fitzgibbon and Young (1994) have emphasised the importance to adults of being identified as dyslexic and being given a clear explanation of what this means. For many individuals it appears that having the label 'dyslexia' or 'specific learning difficulties' is probably an important starting point in helping them to reframe their difficulties.

Assessment and Support

An area of growing concern and major debate at the moment is what kind of support should be offered to students with dyslexia. This is inevitably linked at the individual level to issues about how dyslexia is identified and assessed. Ideally, most people would agree that support should be linked to the particular needs of an individual student based on the severity and nature of their difficulties. In reality, however, many would argue that the methods of assessment in common usage do not necessarily give an accurate prediction of the kind of difficulties encountered in complex reading and writing tasks. Miles (1993), for example, found that among a group of forty-eight clearly identified adults with dyslexia many of them did fairly well on the Schonell R test of single-word recognition. Many widely used reading tests, such as the Neale Analysis of Reading, are designed for children and do not have adequate norms for adults. On top of this, the levels of literacy needed to read academic textbooks and journal articles fluently and accurately enough to extract the meaning are above the average literacy requirements for adults, and are rarely tapped by standard reading tests. A related issue is that some students with dyslexia report that it is the extra effort involved in this type of reading especially, and the consequent fatigue and need for frequent breaks, that is a problem for them. Short periods of testing are not designed to pick up this kind of problem and the subjective experience of effort is a difficult one to quantify. Standardised timed measures of free writing have only been recently developed and are still not widely used, yet it is these complex tasks under timed conditions that probably give the best reflection of the difficulties encountered in the real world. At present, there is no agreement on what tests and information should be routinely used in assessing student and different practitioners use different forms of assessment, thus making it difficult to compare the needs of students. Recent research (Rothstein, 1993; McGuire et al., 1996) in the USA has addressed the issue of what kind of testing is appropriate. In the USA, under Section 504 students with learning disabilities are required to submit documentation verifying their learning disability, although no guidelines are given as to what constitutes adequate documentation. McGuire et al. (1996) state that there is a threefold purpose in doing this.

1. To see if a student is 'otherwise qualified' to meet the admission criteria of a particular institution if given appropriate accommodation for their learning disability. (Accommodation refers to anything that is done to minimise the impact of the student's literacy difficulties on his or her performance. So a student who is slow at writing and who makes many spelling errors may be given extra time to complete an exam, or may be able to dictate their work to a scribe. Once these allowances are made the student would be expected to show the same level of knowledge and understanding of the subject area as other successful students.)
2. To decide on appropriate individual academic accommodation and support for the student.
3. To give the student insight into their own strengths and weaknesses.

In looking at the documentation submitted by 415 students over a 5-year period at one US university, they found that, as in the UK, the nature of the assessment carried out was variable and in general lacked comprehensiveness in that diagnosis was often based on just one psychological test. It was also found that, as in the UK, inappropriate tests were in wide use. The general message seems to be that there needs to be more agreement as to what constitutes good assessment, with wider use of a range of valid and reliable tests. Inevitably, assessment involves a compromise between factors such as practicability, especially in terms of time and expense, and comprehensiveness. The US approach quite explicitly lays responsibility on the student for securing an appropriate assessment and emphasises that the student must be their own advocate.

In the UK a more muddled and patchy mixture of paternalism and self-advocacy seems to operate. Whereas some LEAs (local education authorities) in the UK will pay for students to have an assessment, others will not. Similarly, some LEAs will pay for the support recommended by an assessment, whereas others are reluctant to do so. So students attending the same institution but funded by different LEAs can end up with very different levels of support. Students with dyslexia claim this support from the LEA through applying for the disabled students' allowance. This is an extra grant designed to meet the additional costs of completing the course with a disability. The allowance is divided into several areas so that students can claim up to a certain amount for specialist equipment, such as a word processor or tape recorder, for personal helpers, such as a tutor or reader, and for additional expenses, such as photocopying in the case of a slow reader. The regulations covering the availability of allowances such as these are subject to change, so it is important that students receive up-to-date advice and that there is sufficient publicity about such support so that students with genuine disabilities do not miss out on the support they are entitled to. Many further and higher education institutions in the UK do provide more general support services for students with a range of disabilities, with dyslexia/specific learning difficulties forming the largest category of students with a disability. Support is still patchy, with some institutions providing well-developed services whereas others provide very little, but overall there has been a significant increase in the support services offered over the past 10 years. Among the old universities, the University College North Wales, Bangor, has pioneered support for students with dyslexia and has produced useful books for students with dyslexia and all those involved with teaching them (Miles and Gilroy, 1983; Gilroy, 1993). In setting up institution-based support services some of the same debates that have dominated school-based support for special needs arise. Should support services be focused on a narrow band of students with clearly defined disabilities and if so where and how is the line drawn between those who do or do not get these services? Another approach developed by some institutions is to have support services such as a literacy or reading and writing centre that is open to all students who feel they need it, so that instead of drawing a discrete line disabilities are placed on a continuum. The difficulty with this approach is that it will only work effectively if resources are sufficient for the demands made upon them. Some institutions use a combination of approaches, with some open-access facilities and some facilities specifically for students with identified disabilities. Another debate that spills over from school is where the expertise and responsibility for dyslexia/specific learning difficulties should reside. As in schools, it is argued that all lecturers/tutors should have some understanding of dyslexia and the appropriate support, and at least know whom to contact for further advice. Again the question arises of whose role it is to provide such training and whether it should be mandatory. Other forms of organisational support such as extra time in exams also need to be arranged for some students on the grounds that they need extra writing time and extra time to check over their work. For students with a severe writing disability the use of an amanuensis or a word processor may be considered in exams. At present, there is no consensus about what time allowances should be given in exams, and institutions vary widely in their practice. In addition to support for their specific literacy problems, some students want more general support to address the secondary problems of low self-esteem or anxiety, especially if they have encountered many negative experiences. Self-help groups and the chance to meet other students with similar problems are important to some students. Such support can help students address the more general problems of how you cope with a disability and share examples of successful coping strategies. More subtle issues such as the ethos of the department and the attitude of the student's lecturers and peers to dyslexia can also have an impact on how that individual will fare. Given the wide range of literacy difficulties that students with dyslexia can encounter and the attendant secondary problems, it is hardly surprising that for some students a complex package of support is called for.

Chapter 2
Overview of the Study

In this chapter we give general information about the empirical aspects of the project and report some of the other data we gathered. We hope this will help the reader put the interviews into context. Our description will be fairly informal and we will report only our main findings, because more formal, comprehensive treatments of the material are currently in preparation. The aim of this chapter is therefore to provide the reader with a flavour of the similarities and differences between the dyslexics we studied and a matched group of students with no evident problem.

The dyslexic participants, with one exception, were all university students, attending a new university, which, at the time of the study, was in the middle range with respect to the support it provided. Like many institutions, it was in the process of developing its services and while the study was being done a literacy-support centre was opened and a special-needs adviser appointed. Despite this, such services were not widely known about in the institution and there was considerable departmental variation in the response to dyslexia. The participants were contacted, in the first instance, through Student Services. They were told that the aim of the project was to identify problems experienced by adult student dyslexics with a view to improving facilities, and were given general information about the probable demands on their time and the nature of their participation. If, on the basis of this, they agreed to participate they contacted Steven Morgan, research assistant on the project, for further details and to arrange testing times. They were then told as much as possible about the tasks, tests and interviews, and only information that we thought might influence their performance was withheld. For example, we did not tell them that the psychometric tests measured anxiety and self-esteem. The participants were seen over three sessions, each lasting about an hour and were paid for their time. At the end of their participation they were fully debriefed. Early on in their participation they were asked to nominate a friend or acquaintance of the same gender, on the same course and of approximately the same age, who would serve as a control participant. They were assured that their performance would not be directly compared with this person because we were only interested in comparing group performance. They were also assured of the anonymity and confidentiality of their individual results. We explained that although the results might be published, they, as individuals, would in no way be identified or identifiable. However, before embarking on this book, which clearly violates this contract by reporting highly personal information about individuals, we contacted all those who appear here for their permission to publish.

Although we tested many more, we collected a full set of data from 16 dyslexic students and 16 students with no known problem (the control group), who were matched with the dyslexics, pairwise, for gender and, as far as possible, age and degree course. The dyslexics were all students who were registered as such with the university authorities, having been required to provide documentary evidence of their disability. To participate they also had to score four or more on the Adult Dyslexia Checklist (more of this later). There were nine males and seven females in each group. The average ages for dyslexics and controls were 26 years and 23 years old respectively. Arts, science and social science degrees were all represented in both samples. Fourteen of each group were in the first or second year of the degree, one in the third year, and one on a pre-university course. See Table 1 for further details.

The dyslexic participants were seen in three sessions. In the first they were asked to write an essay, in the second to fill in three questionnaires, and in the third to participate in an interview. The control participants were seen in two sessions because they were not interviewed. The purpose of the writing task was to identify the kinds of error that might mark dyslexic students as a group apart from their peers. That they might make more spelling errors seemed obvious. Less predictable was the question of whether they would also make more grammatical errors. The purpose of the questionnaires was to gather information related to personality and educational experiences. One of the questionnaires measured self-esteem, which we thought might well be lower in our dyslexic sample. As we see from the interviews, dyslexics are so frequently the subject of low expectations and even derision that this seemed a reasonable expectation. A second questionnaire measured

Table 1: Some characteristics of participants in the study

Number/name of participant	Age (years)	Gender (m/f)	Father's/Mother's occupation	Course	Left school (years)	'O' levels or similar	'A' levels or similar	Dyslexia Checklist 0–12	Self-esteem	Trait anxiety	State anxiety	Spelling errors (%)
Dyslexic Participants												
D1. Andy	30	m	Engineer	soc sci	17	5	2	12	VL	H	VH	31
D2. Janet	28	f	Accountant	soc sci	16	8	0	5	I	I	I	5
D3. Sean	23	m	Sales rep.	sci	18	8	0	12	L	H	I	3
D4. June	41	f	Manual worker	soc sci	16	4	0	5	L	I	I	11
D5. Henry	25	m	Scientist	sci	16	3	0	8	VL	I	I	8
D6. Caroline	19	f	Teacher	soc sci	18	9	0	9	L	I	I	3
D7. Peter	42	m	Manager	arts	15	0	0	6	L	I	I	7
D8. Jenny	22	f	Accountant	soc sci	18	10	?	11	L	H	H	3
D9. Patrick	24	m	Musician	sci	19	?	3	6	VH	I	I	12
D10	18	m	Lecturer	sci	18	6	3	8	I	I	I	9
D11	18	m	Ship's officer	sci	18	8	4	9	I	I	I	9
D12	19	f	Property business	soc sci	18	8	5	4	L	I	I	1
D13	20	f	General worker	arts	19	7	3	8	L	I	I	1
D14	20	f	Designer	arts	18	10	5	11	I	I	I	5
D15	24	m	Teacher	arts	18	7	2	10	I	I	I	5
D16	20	m	?	arts	19	6	2	9	I	I	I	17
Control Participants												
C1	21	f	Lecturer	soc sci	18	8	3	1	VH	I	I	1
C2	20	f	Teacher	arts	18	8	3	4	VH	I	I	1
C3	19	f	Lecturer	arts	18	9	4	0	VH	I	I	1
C4	22	m	Judge	soc sci	18	9	3	4	H	I	L	1
C5	31	f	Railway worker	soc sci	18	4	3	1	H	I	I	2
C6	22	f	Civil Service	sci	18	8	0	2	I	I	I	2
C7	35	m	Air Force	soc sci	16	4	0	4	L	I	I	1
C8	27	m	Engineer	arts	18	0	0	2	H	I	I	2
C9	22	m	Truck driver	sci	16	7	2	1	L	I	I	2
C10	20	f	Solicitor	soc sci	18	8	3	3	I	I	I	0
C11	20	m	?	arts	18	9	4	1	I	I	I	0
C12	20	f	Managing director	arts	16	9	2	3	H	I	I	0
C13	21	f	Administrator	soc sci	18	10	0	3	H	I	H	1
C14	24	m	Engineer	soc sci	19	6	4	0	L	VH	I	0
C15	20	m	Computer engineer	sci	18	9	2	3	VH	I	I	1
C16	21	m	Driving instructor	soc sci	19	8	2	0	VH	I	I	0

Key: (1) Anxiety and self-esteem: VH = very high; H = high; I = intermediate; L = low; VL = very low.
(2) Where father's occupation is not available mother's occupation is given. In some cases neither was available.

anxiety, of both trait and state varieties (trait anxiety refers to a pervasive, persistent level of anxiety that is a general characteristic of the person; state anxiety refers to the level of anxiety experienced at the time of testing). We reasoned that, given their many trials and tribulations over a lifetime, dyslexics might well have greater general and specific levels of anxiety. The third questionnaire was constructed by the research team to gather information about educational experiences and perceptions of the future. We reasoned that qualifications, subject likes and dislikes, perceptions of their own ability and future plans were likely to be adversely affected by a disability that is frequently mistaken for stupidity or laziness by others. More of this shortly.

The Tests and Tasks

The Adult Dyslexia Checklist

This is a screening test devised by Michael Vinegrad of The Adult Dyslexia Association (a copy may be obtained from the World Wide Web at: http://www.futurenet.co.uk/charity/ado/check.html). It consists of 20 questions and was standardised on a sample of 679 adults (aged 16–68, mainly students), of whom some were known to be dyslexic. Using various statistical procedures, 12 of these questions were found to be best at discriminating the dyslexics from the rest of the sample. Examples of these questions are 'When writing cheques, do you frequently find yourself making mistakes?', 'Is your spelling poor?', and 'Did you find it hard to learn your multiplication tables at school?'. For our purposes, we counted only those of these 12 questions that were responded to positively: the more of these questions that are answered in the affirmative the greater is the indication of dyslexia. More than nine positive responses is regarded as a very severe impairment.

Essay writing

This part of the investigation was conducted largely by Catherine Matthews, a psychology undergraduate, as the basis for her final year dissertation. Each participant was asked to write an essay about their life as a student. We selected this topic because of its undemanding nature, and because we assumed that all participants would have equally rich experiences which they would find equally easy to relate in writing. They were given 35 minutes for the task and were obliged to spend the first 5 minutes in planning the essay. To standardise content and help them in their planning they were given guidelines about the kind of information we were looking for (e.g. information about their course, accommodation, friends, leisure etc). The remaining half hour was for writing and was split into three 10-minutes periods, signalled by an alarm (a loud but not distracting bleep). Participants were asked to mark the point in the essay they had reached when the alarm rang. This provided us with a basis for assessing their output per minute during the first, middle and last thirds of essay writing. They were asked to think of this essay as being done under examination conditions.

The Culture Free Self-Esteem Inventory – Form AD (adults) (Battle, 1992, 2nd edition)

This took approximately 10 minutes to complete. There is a total of 40 items, split into 4 sections. The first is concerned with General Self-Esteem (16 items) and refers to the individual's overall perception of his/her self-worth. It includes questions such as 'Do you feel you are as important as most people?', 'Do you often feel ashamed of yourself?', and 'Are you usually successful when you attempt important tasks or assignments?'. The second section is concerned with Social Self-Esteem (eight items), being the aspect of self-esteem that refers to an individual's perceptions of the quality of relationship with peers. Sample questions are 'Do you have only a few friends?', 'Are you as intelligent as most people?', and 'Do most people respect your views?'. The third section is concerned with Personal Self-Esteem (eight items), the aspect that refers to the individual's most intimate perceptions of self-worth. Sample questions are 'Are you easily depressed?', 'Are your feelings easily hurt?', and 'Do you worry a lot?'. Finally, there is a 'Lie' section (eight items) to detect defensiveness. These questions measure the respondent's willingness to admit to socially undesirable behaviours, and the more of these she admits to the less defensive is the person. Sample questions are 'Have you ever taken anything that didn't belong to you?', 'Do you gossip at times?', and 'Do you ever lie?'. Standardisation of the CFSEI (Culture Free Self-Esteem Inventory) test has produced a scale for the combined scores of the first three sections, which classifies respondents into very high, high, intermediate, low and very low self-esteem. We shall use this classification for our sample. On the Lie (defensiveness) subtest, 92% of respondents admitted to four or more socially undesirable behaviours, so we can regard a score of four or more as being the norm.

The State-Trait Anxiety Inventory (Speilberger et al., 1970).

This took approximately 10 minutes. It consists of 2 sections of 20 questions each, one measuring trait anxiety and the other state anxiety. Trait anxiety refers to relatively stable individual differences in anxiety-proneness. People differ in their tendency to respond to stressful situations as dangerous or threatening and to respond to such situation with increases in anxiety. This underlying, personality-related proneness to anxiety is measured using a number of statements such as 'I feel nervous and restless', to which the respondent has to indicate how often they generally feel this way: almost always, often, sometimes or almost never. State anxiety refers to the presence of the emotional state of anxiety, characterised by subjective feelings of tension, apprehension, nervousness and worry, at a given moment in time and at a particular level of intensity. It is measured using statements similar to those used for trait anxiety (e.g. 'I feel nervous'), but this time the respondent has to indicate how intensely they feel this was at that particular moment in time: very much so, moderately so, somewhat or not at all. The two concepts are related in that an individual with high trait anxiety will experience state anxiety more intensely and more frequently. Standardisation of the test by its author has produced norms for both trait and state anxiety, and in this investigation we have used these norms to produce our own classificatory levels of anxiety defined thus: very high (scores more than two standard deviations from the mean), high (between one and two standard deviations more than the mean), intermediate (less than one standard deviation more than or less than the mean), low (between one and two standard deviations less than the mean), and very low (scores less than two standard deviations from the mean). Each member of our sample is put into one of these five categories.

The Academic and Professional Profile questionnaire

This was constructed by the research team. It was piloted and revised before administration and took about 25 minutes to complete. It consists of five sections: Biographical Information, At School, Between School and University, At University, The Future. The purpose of the questionnaire was to get structured information from both dyslexic and control participants which could then be compared. The questions were formulated to try to trace salient aspects of the participants' educational history from primary school to university. In particular, we were concerned with their opinions about how they thought they compared with their peers, with respect to academic ability, written expression, anxiety and so on. To a large extent, the questions mirrored those asked in the interview, but, although less comprehensive than the interview, have the advantage of allowing us to compare the dyslexics with matched non-dyslexics. We deal with some of the questions asked in the next section. The full questionnaire is reproduced in the Appendix.

Results

In this section we report selected results from the three question-naires, dealing largely with the replies to the Academic and Profes-sional Profile (APP) questionnaire we supplement these, where appropriate, with data from the psychometric tests of anxiety and self-esteem.

In this section, as in the writing tasks and the interviews them-selves, perhaps the single most significant feature is the large differ-ences between dyslexic participants: differences in the severity of their impairment, differences in their writing and spelling ability and differences in their experiences, their attitudes and the attitudes of others. These differences will become evident in the interviews. For now, we are concerned with the overall picture.

The Adult Dyslexia Checklist (ADC) revealed a clear overall difference between the two groups of participants. However, there was some overlap between the two groups, with two controls and one dyslexic subject producing a score of four, the cut-off point for select-ing the dyslexic group. The overlap may, of course, have been greater if we had not used a cut-off. Although the ADC is a screening test, and therefore somewhat lacking the sensitivity to discriminate small differences, this is the first of several results that suggest a grey diag-nostic area between dyslexia and the rest of the population. However, we also see from Table 1 that several of dyslexics were severely impaired (scores greater than eight). Some of these were interviewed.

We were concerned to discover when our dyslexics had been perceived as having a problem (not necessarily recognised as dyslexia), and whether they had received remedial attention. Fifteen were identified as having a problem when at school, but only 10 of these ever received remedial attention, usually in the form of extra tuition with reading and spelling. Of these 15, 9 were identified early (when at primary school) but only 4 were given extra help at the time. Two of the control group were identified as having problems at primary school (one with a literacy problem, the other with a vision problem), neither of whom seems to have been given any specific remedial help, and they seem to have subsequently 'recovered'.

We reasoned that dyslexics' disability should have been manifest in their school performance, particularly in subjects such as English. Accordingly, we asked them to nominate the subject or subjects they had done worse at when at school. At primary school, both groups tended to nominate English, maths, or both, as being their worst subject, but whereas English tended to be the greater problem for dyslexics, the controls reported a greater problem with maths. In secondary school, where there is a greater range of subjects, the dyslexics' problems with English was even more marked, whereas the controls' problems were more evenly spread across subjects.

We asked participants if they thought their written work underestimated their true ability. The picture was clear: almost all the dyslexics considered their written work to be worse than their true ability, both at primary school and at secondary school. The control group were much less negative about their written work.

We asked participants to rate how they thought they had compared, academically, with their peers when at school. We reasoned that, because of their disability, they probably considered themselves worse. This was clearly found to be the case. At both primary and secondary school almost all the dyslexics had considered themselves academically weaker than their peers. This was not the case for the control group, almost all of whom considered themselves to be about average. This result suggests that dyslexics' had poorer self-esteem during their school years than the members of the control group.

Given this general picture of perceptions during the school years we may reasonably expect that dyslexics were more anxious than their peers when at school. When asked this question the difference between dyslexics and controls was marked. Dyslexics consistently considered themselves to have been more anxious than their peers whereas controls considered themselves to have been about average.

In the British education system most students acquire nationally taken pre-university examinations of two types/levels. The first set of these public examinations ('O' levels or equivalent) are usually taken when about 16 years old. The second set are usually taken when about 18 years old ('A' levels or equivalent). However, both can be taken at any time. University entry is usually based on performance in these examinations, particularly the latter, although special dispensation is given if the applicant is mature or has documented special needs. Both dyslexics and controls left school at the same average age (17 years 7 months approximately). A minority of both groups came directly to university whereas the remainder began their degree three (controls) or four (dyslexics) years later. (No importance should be attached to this similarity as it is a direct consequence of our matching the two groups for age.) These intervening years were spent working and/or collecting educational qualifications from another institution such as a college of higher education. At the time of entry to university 14 dyslexics and 16 controls had GCSEs or equivalent, whereas 9 dyslexics and 11 controls had 'A' levels or equivalent. In general, the controls were better qualified than the dyslexics.

Participants were asked which aspect of their degree course they were worst at. Because of the diverse nature of the courses and the consequently diverse answers, we classified their replies into written aspects and practical aspects. Of the 14 dyslexics who replied to this question, the majority (12) cited written aspects of their course. The replies of the control group were comparable, in that of the 12 who replied 9 also cited the written aspects. This is a little puzzling, given that 14 of the 15 dyslexics who were asked whether they had any special problems at university replied in the affirmative and for 8 of these the problem was severe enough to warrant the acceptance of remedial help. (None of the controls said they had a special problem.) This suggests that the dyslexics' disability does not seem to be affecting their written work. However, this conclusion is probably wrong. Students generally choose a degree course that interests them and that reflects their strengths rather than their weaknesses, so problematic areas would tend to be only a small component of the course. Furthermore, written work is usually a cornerstone of assessment in most degree programmes. These two observations suggest that a safer interpretation may simply be that all students consider written work to be their weakness, but because the question was a relative question ('which is your worst subject?') the differences are not evident. This conclusion is supported by the fact that dyslexics considered their written work to underestimate their true ability. The control group did not consider this to be the case to the same extent.

When asked how they compared academically with their student peers, dyslexics rated themselves as being worse, suggesting the persistence of the low self-esteem found during the school years. On the question of perceived relative anxiety, dyslexics again considered themselves to be more anxious than their student peers whereas the effect was much less marked in the control group.

This is a convenient point to report the results of the psychometric assessments of self-esteem and anxiety. To a large degree, the results supported the results from the APP questionnaire. Dyslexics' scores on the Culture Free Self-Esteem Inventory indicated clearly lower self-esteem than for the control group (see Table 1). Furthermore, the ' Lie' subscale of the inventory revealed that the dyslexics were more defensive than the controls. They were, in general, less willing to admit to socially undesirable behaviours, which may be taken as evidence of lower self-esteem. On the question of anxiety, although the dyslexics tended to produce higher anxiety scores on the State-Trait Anxiety Inventory (see Table 1), the difference was not statistically significant. We think the reason for this is that dyslexics' anxiety may only be higher in situations specifically related to their disability such as essay writing and exams. This needs further investigation.

In the final part of the questionnaire we were looking for evidence that dyslexics' perception of the future, in terms of their career, had always been significantly affected by their disability. We asked them what career they had anticipated when at school, and expected to find dyslexics either avoiding jobs in which literacy was important or having no career plans. There was indeed some evidence for this. Five dyslexics, compared with seven controls, cited careers in which literacy is important (medicine, teaching). In addition, six dyslexics, compared with three controls, had not considered their future career when at school. When asked when they had first considered going to university the two groups did not differ. Finally, when asked what, if anything, might prevent them from achieving their career ambition, five dyslexics cited either their disability or a lack of confidence. Only one control cited poor confidence as the reason. The remaining reasons involved insufficient qualifications or other reasons such as sexism or lack of money.

We turn now to the results of the writing task. There is much anecdotal evidence to suggest that dyslexics have a problem constructing grammatical sentences and this is evident from some of the interviews. Some of the participants report that tutors complain about both their grammar and their spelling. These reports are given credence by the evidence for short-term memory impairment which predicts that dyslexics may well have problems holding the words, phrases and clauses of complex sentences in memory while writing. We decided to look into this. The problem, however, is the difficulty in measuring the grammaticality of sentences. We are currently looking at ways in which to measure this but in the meantime have resorted to cruder indicators of grammatical problems. We looked firstly at essay length, reasoning that grammatical problems would slow writing even when the content was simple. We did find evidence of slowing, with the dyslexic group producing essays that were approximately 100 words shorter than those of the controls. Furthermore, the difference in output was consistent over three time periods, suggesting a constant, underlying problem with no differential fatigue effects. The problem with interpreting this output difference in terms of grammatical impairment is that it could also be due to the dyslexics' poor spelling. They could have written less because of the greater time being spent on spelling rather than because of a difficulty in sentence construction. Accordingly, we then looked at sentence length, reasoning that dyslexics might well write longer, poorly structured sentences. However, there was no evidence of this. Indeed, dyslexics' sentences were, if anything, shorter. This could of course be a deliberate strategy, used to compensate for the problem. This was almost certainly true of the most impaired participant (Andy), who wrote very short, very simple sentences. The question of whether dyslexics have a problem with sentence construction remains to be answered.

Dyslexia is virtually defined in terms of problems at the lexical level, in single-word reading and spelling. We carried out an extensive analysis of spelling errors, only the main findings of which we report here. Firstly, as expected, dyslexics made many more errors (6% of all words) than the controls (1% of all words) but, as we said in our caveat earlier, there were considerable individual differences. We see from Table 1 that the proportion of misspelt words for the control group was consistently very small (around 1%) but that the dyslexics varied from 1% to a maximum of 31% (see Table 1). We then classified these errors into categories that cast some light on the nature of the problem. A full analysis and interpretation, currently in preparation, is complex and needs many qualifications. All we can do here is to draw a few general conclusions.

Our first category of spelling error brought together those errors that did not preserve the consonant–vowel structure of the word. We reasoned that because dyslexics have a well-documented problem with the awareness of the sound structure of words and with verbal short-term memory they should produce a large number of these errors. It is not a homogeneous category because we think that the precise origins vary, but they have in common the feature that the sound structure has been lost. Examples of this category are *lagrel* (largely), *caraterig* (catering), *intimidaing* (intimidating), and *leth* (length). In some cases (e.g. *power* (pure) and *can* (kind) the target has become confused with another word with a slightly different sound structure. The structure of these errors does suggest a problem with identifying, holding and then accurately transcribing the component sounds of the words. However, contrary to expectation, they were few in number, accounting for only 14% of all errors. We are currently looking into this.

A second major category consisted of words in which one phoneme (component sound) and only one phoneme had been misspelt. This was the most numerous category, accounting for 56% of all errors. Again, this is not a homogeneous category because the kind of misspelling varies. In some cases the participant has misspelt a consonant (*cource* (course)), in another a rule has been violated (*citys* (cities)), in a third the consonant has not been doubled (*dificult* (difficult)), in a fourth an irregular word has been misspelt (*parms* (palms)), and so on. The importance of this general category of error is, firstly, that a single phoneme is involved. This implies that these dyslexics are capable of breaking words down into their component sounds, contrary to the notion that they have problems with phonological awareness. The second important aspect of this category is that it identifies a major problem with knowledge of sound–spelling correspondences and with the many factors that govern the spelling of English (not known for its regularity). Noteworthy is the fact that whereas many people misspell relatively infrequent irregular words, these dyslexics misspelt many common irregular words (e.g. *frend* (friend), *yong* (young)).

The third major category of error was lexical, consisting of misspellings which themselves were words. In contrast to the lexical errors we reported earlier, where the sound structure of the error was slightly different from that of the target (e.g. *can* (kind)), in this category the consonant–vowel structure of error and target were the same (e.g. *to* (too), *of* (off), *their* (there)), suggesting that the problem is one of remembering the appropriate spelling of the word in question.

The Interviews

Finally, we turn to the focus of this book. In a third session, the dyslexics, and only the dyslexics, were the subject of a semi-structured interview. In these interviews we were concerned with the experience of being dyslexic, with educational experiences at school and at university, and with the attitudes of our sample and the attitudes of significant others, such as teachers and parents.

The interview was divided into three sets of questions: past experiences with dyslexia, present difficulties faced at university, and a short section on future goals and expectations. An early version of the interview was piloted on two participants who do not appear in the current sample and on the basis of this various amendments were made. The questions were always general to begin with, to give the interviewee the opportunity to speak freely, and then, depending on the detail in the reply, more probing, to illuminate issues of specific interest. Sometimes, when a participant's unique experiences suggested a particularly fruitful line of inquiry supplementary questions were asked. The result of this semi-structured format is a combination of standardised information, gathered from all participants, and revelations that are participant-specific and depend on the personality and memory of the individual. We hope you will agree that this strategy has produced interesting and informative interviews.

The first section focused on participants' experiences and difficulties at primary and secondary school. In addition to the nature and severity of the intellectual difficulties experienced we were particularly interested in the attitudes of parents and teachers to the participant. Was, for example, the problem recognised or was the interviewee regarded as lazy or stupid? Did the school and/or parents provide support of either an educational or an emotional kind? Related to this were questions about the participant's perception of himself/herself. How did he/she cope with the problem and with the attitudes of others and did diagnosis change the nature of the dyslexic experience?

The second section pursued these major themes for the participants' time at university. Again, we were concerned with specific problems such as note-taking, essays and examinations and the ways in which the participant coped with these problems. We were concerned with whether they had to adopt specific strategies to deal with their problems and whether word processors and other technological aids had proved helpful. In addition, we were interested in the constellation of everyday problems reported by dyslexics: filling in forms, writing cheques and reading timetables. We also questioned participants on the attitudes of their peers and of their university tutors who, because they were aware of the participant's diagnosis, could not be excused negative attitudes on the grounds of ignorance. Most importantly, we were interested in the participants' perception of themselves, particularly with respect to their self-esteem.

Finally, the last few questions were aimed at revealing the participants' expectations of the future, especially with respect to the anticipated effects of being dyslexic on their career prospects.

Participants were fully informed about the nature and purpose of the interview. They were told that the session would take about 45 minutes and that it would be taped for transcription and possible publication in journal articles or a book on dyslexia. They were paid for their participation in all three sessions of the investigation. The interviews were carried out in the quiet but somewhat austere surroundings of the psychological laboratories by Steven Morgan, the research assistant on the project, who is himself dyslexic. We believe this, and Steve's enthusiasm, contributed to the frankness with which participants spoke and the degree to which they were prepared to reveal quite intimate and often distressing aspects of their dyslexic experience. The interviews were transcribed by a professional audio typist who was instructed to 'smooth over' the false starts, 'ums' and 'ahs', and many other imperfections so prevalent in normal conversation. We believe that the result, although thus sanitised, captures the essence of what was said.

We report the interviews of 9 of the 16 participants. These were chosen to present as diverse and comprehensive a coverage as possible of the experiences encountered by students with dyslexia. So the students selected are from traditional and non-traditional academic backgrounds, arts, social-science and science degrees, relatively high and low literacy requirement courses, direct entry and mature students, different social and economic backgrounds, male and female, severe and less severe difficulties, early and late identification of dyslexia, and good and poor support for their difficulties. In each interview chapter we begin with a quote from the interview that we think captures a significant aspect of the participant's experience. We then report the interview and finish with informal comments by the authors. These comments should not be taken as a clinical analysis of the individual, for which a much more rigorous and structured investigation would be required. They are merely our opinion on salient aspects of the individual's experience.

Chapter 3
Andy

'School, to be perfectly frank, was absolutely a disaster from the word go.'

Andy was a 27-year-old student taking a part-time degree in Law. He received the maximum score of 12 on the Adult Dyslexia Checklist, and his performance on the free-writing task confirmed that he was one of the most severely dyslexic students in the group studied. On the Culture Free Self-Esteem Inventory his score fell into the very low category.

The Interview

School, to be frank, was absolutely a disaster from the word go. But I suppose it starts before that, the reason being that I was brought up by my grandmother, who was very old and who's recently died. She had very, very intelligent brothers, and they were all capable of reading and writing before they went to school. So she tried to teach me, she did so much, but she said I was the most frustrating person to teach, nothing going in, I didn't look as if I was paying attention and whatever she wrote down was coming out completely different, and she was, you know, 'what is wrong with him?'

Then I went to school and the first memory, I suppose, of infant school is being distanced. What I mean by that is not being able to really relate to what was happening; it was a very frustrating experience and there was a lot of anger with that. I was fine with creative things, I was good at music, but when it came to writing I had difficulty holding the pens, and I was actually flipping from hand to hand and I was told I had to use one hand. It got to the stage where the teacher put a crepe bandage around my left hand and tied it to the chair, and that was in infant school. Then there was a sense of fear. But then very early on, I think heading into junior school, there was this idea I was stupid, people had actually said to my grandmother within my hearing distance, 'He's terribly slow, I don't think he's going to do very much'.

At that age, being put under pressure from my grandmother and also my parents, I was starting to feel an absolute failure, and it started there.

Junior school was very difficult; I was being bullied. I was always in the bottom group; I could understand what was going on, but I couldn't get it down on paper. One of my lasting memories of junior school is that I produced a piece of work which looked fine to me and after the lunch break the teacher came back to the class and said: 'Everyone's done a wonderful bit of work except for one person and that person is Andy and I want him to come out and hold up his book so the rest of the class can see it'. So I dragged myself up and again this feeling of being so small, so stupid, I held up my work, I didn't know what was wrong with it and the whole class gasped.

I take it the school wouldn't recognise dyslexia?

No, I was stupid, and boarding school after that was exactly the same. I was caned frequently.

Did they put you in remedial or extra classes?

Not in the state sector. When I went to boarding school I had extra tuition, which was more of the same, it was not specialist help.

Did that help?

No, not at all. ... They turned round and said that you were lazy ... lazy, stupid ... because you had the contrast of probably performing quite well in lessons verbally ... I was quite capable of performing well orally and never being able to produce the goods on paper or in exams; it was a nightmare. School reports always used to say things like 'intelligent to converse with but', and there was always that 'but'. So they presumed you were lazy because you were not performing up to the set standard.

Did your parents recognise that you had difficulties at all?

They didn't really, not at all [silence].

In general, do you feel your family have been supportive or unsupportive to you in dealing with your dyslexia?

No, but I don't think they ever understood what it was. My grandmother was wonderful about it, but my mother and father, no, not really.

Is there an incidence of dyslexia in the family at all?

My father had a definite problem reading. I noticed he never wrote to me when I was at school. I never saw him write anything down; he always used his secretary.

What age were you when you were assessed?

I was 18 or 19 ... It was quite late on. I had left school and I worked a while for Marks and Spencer's, which was absolutely mind-numbingly boring. I knew I wasn't possibly as stupid as everyone made out. I inherited a little bit of money and I went to a crammer (private college) in Oxford, and that was to do 'A' and 'O' level resits. It was there that one of the tutors said 'you have a problem, you've really got a problem'; then they sent me to a psychologist.

Before you were assessed, what did you think of yourself and why did you think you were having difficulties?

I had serious problems with self-esteem and how I felt about myself; I mean it was not a minor thing, I was very withdrawn. I had an interest in all sorts of things, I still do, but at the back of my mind there is this voice saying, 'you're not really capable, forget it', and that was always there.

Did knowing you were dyslexic change the way you saw yourself and did this have any effect on your academic work or your relationships with other people?

It had a name; I wasn't stupid, the psychologist said I wasn't stupid and it was a lovely feeling. I thought, I can probably get some form of help and carry on studying and do what I want to do. I actually had a sense of purpose for the first time, which was wonderful.

Did you receive any additional help after the assessment and do you think it helped you?

From the state sector no, but I met a wonderful lady in Oxford, who has been wonderful, and she helped me and she said, 'I can see you're bright'.

What kind of help was that?

It was sounds, a lot of writing practice, helping to form letters, allowing me to take my time, teaching me mnemonics, techniques for remembering. The biggest thing was to tell me to find a level I was happy at when I was reading and also saying there was no really right way to do it, what was right for me was going to work and little tips like using a pointer or a pencil help me cope.

How is your reading?

It is very slow, when I'm approached with closely written stuff I like to put a card underneath to block out the words underneath so that my eyes aren't strained and then I'll point [to the words], but the more tired I get the more difficult it is. So in some sense you'll be looking at a page of text and you may be jumping ahead, or skipping a line, that's what I find ... I do jump ahead, I do skip a line, then I realise I'm reading a line I've already read and that produces a sense of absolute rage and frustration. You have to read a page two or three times before you extract anything ... it's difficult, it's a slog.

Why did you choose to study here?

I wanted to do a part-time course in Law and it had to be close to home, and this was the ideal place to come for me. That was the main reason, but the other one was that it took me so long to read things, if I was on a full-time course I would quickly go under. The part-time course allows work at my own pace and allows me to work as hard or be as lazy as I want. The reading is very difficult; I get my girlfriend to read a lot to me. The thing that really annoys me is writing an essay each week, to get it back with a decent mark then find the spelling ringed; it's so infuriating.

How does it affect your self-esteem, how does it affect your determination: does it make you more determined to overcome that particular problem or do you sometimes feel like throwing it in the bin, to say I've had enough?

There are times I feel like that, but, after saying that, I'm very critical with my own work. We can relate this back to school and no matter what I do it's never good enough. I feel that this is something I'm imposing on myself, but it has overtones of the past coming through loud and clear. I'm recognising it more and more; it is never good enough, never ever good enough.

Do you think that the problems that you face at university are much the same as other student's?

Whether this is a problem or an unshared neurosis I don't know, but I never feel as good as anyone else on the course. I find it particularly difficult in seminars or in class when we are given a handout to actually follow it and know that everyone else has read it. It often happens where I'm halfway down the first page where everyone else has read it and taken it in and I feel totally out of it, and then I think if I can't read it I shouldn't be here. ... There are times in the library if I had a white stick and a guide dog I wouldn't feel so bad, there are times when I can't find something and I can't find it for looking for it, and everything is blending into one and I'm thinking where the devil is it? Then I go and ask the librarian and on several occasions they have been really rude and said it is on the shelf, all you have to do is look. The other thing is I'm on a limited income, and in some cases photocopying is not an added bonus for dyslexic students, it's a must, and I spend a fortune on photocopying things and enlarging things and I think the institution should make that available free of charge. When I approached the LEA [local education authority] I asked if I was able to receive anything, they said there was nothing available for part-time students, and I don't know what is available, there is no information made easily available.

Have you told any of your tutors about your difficulties?

My course leader knows because I handed in my assessment and he showed no emotion. ... He made arrangements for me to dictate my exams, which has been great, for exam work. I noticed he had taken time to photocopy and enlarge something for me and I'm very grateful to him. There are just two course tutors who know, one because I wanted to do very much an exam to try out my techniques that I had tried to refine since the summer and I said, 'Do you mind if I use my word processor if I come in and do it?', and he said, 'That's fine', but the look of horror on his face.

Are you receiving any support for your dyslexia [at university]?

No. ... In my first year I asked FA [learning-support tutor] for information on how to go about writing essays and that sort of thing, and she spent a lot of time with me and that is the help I have had.

Ideally, what sort of support do you think should be available for dyslexic students?

I'd like to meet some other dyslexic students; that would be helpful. You're asking a very difficult person, because I'm used to coping on my own and that's what I do best. I think I would love to be able to take part in some classes that would help give me memory techniques. I'd also like someone generally to help deal with the volume of work that there is and help me organise it, help me work out a plan.

What aspects of your work do you feel you do well in?

None of it, but that's kind of down to self-confidence, which I'm trying to build up. Meeting other dyslexic students would perhaps help me in my confidence.

What strategies have you found effective in helping you deal with your work?

Because law is such a vast subject, what I've done from day one, I went out and got the past exam papers and looked at them to find out which questions were coming up regularly. Followed very closely my seminar booklets, realised they weren't going to examine us on anything really other than what was there and each subject seminar; there were eight separate units within the group so I concentrated for revision on five of each of them and it worked. For memory, I used the Buzan techniques for remembering the number images. The best example I can give you is the tort of negligence in a case called Donaghue and Stephenson, it's number two on my list and number two is a swan and I have said swan's belonging to Mr Donaghue live in a neighbourhood principal, it doesn't make sense to anyone other than me but it works. And I remember extracts from cases by beating a rhythm, and that's some-thing I've taught myself. Then I make lists of cases for particular sections of my work, e.g. I'm interested in horse racing, so for each area I've constructed a race format, so for negligence there are four runners, duty, breech, damage, causation, then they are categorised for numbers so duty has five to one, which means there are five cases which I must remember, breech has four to one.

Do you use any form of technology, and how useful do you find it?

I have my word processor. I wouldn't be without it.

How do you find the spellchecker?

Well, yesterday I was checking something and the word 'principal' came up and there were two forms of spelling and I'd chosen the wrong one. Misspelling places and names I just can't help; some words are so weird it just doesn't pick them up at all or if it does I will not even attempt to use it.

How do you think your particular personality influences the way you deal with dyslexia, or has dyslexia had an influence on how your personality has developed?

As a child I was very, very withdrawn; after I was assessed I realised there was a problem, and it was all linked with not being stupid, but also linked to not being a terribly good person because of being stupid. And when I started to do law the immediate thing was, you really shouldn't be here, they'd made a hell of a mistake letting me on the course, but perhaps they haven't made a mistake and I'm doing it and really enjoying it. I had a nervous breakdown and I got terribly depressed and I was hospitalised; that was just after I started the course before Christmas last year.

Do you think a support service would have helped?

I think that would have been a long shot; the key problem was that I had lost my self-confidence, I was finding it very difficult and I was coping with memories of school, and it was bad, really bad. It's little things, for example, when I go to church and someone asks me to read I make up an excuse like, I've forgotten my reading glasses, and yet I haven't. If they want me to read I must have it at least a week before so that I can partially memorise it.

Is that what you did at school as well?

No, in school I always made myself terribly ill before exams, especially in boarding school so that I would spend the time in the sanatorium; when I say make myself ill I mean drink lots of salty water, doing really silly things, anything to get out of it. I actually ran away from boarding school, which was just to get away, it was horrible and it was not a happy time.

Do you tell other students that you're dyslexic?

No, just my girlfriend.

At what stage did you tell her?

I borrowed ten pounds from her and I gave her a cheque and it looked as if something had crawled across it, and she said, 'what is the problem?'

Do you ever ask other students or staff for specific help i.e. proofreading a piece of work?

I always ask my girlfriend to read my work.

Are there any situations that you find particularly difficult or embarrassing because of your dyslexia?

Reading train timetables, I missed the train the other day because of reading it incorrectly, reading signposts in the car, and I simply don't know my right from my left and that is infuriating to everyone in the car. My girlfriend now says this is my side and that's your side, and I find that quite humiliating at times. The other thing is when someone gives me something to read and I say I have read it, but I haven't taken it in; writing cheques, thank God for switch cards.

Have you ever felt isolated at university or when you were younger because of your dyslexia?

It's a self-imposed isolation with me because I haven't told many people on the course; two friends whom I sit with, they know, but I haven't told anyone else. I don't want to be called stupid. I worked for a charity before coming to university, I was lucky because they set me up as a fund-raiser; I was very good at that, I used a secretary to write letters. I had to leave a note for my boss's husband and it was the only occasion I did it and the man was absolutely foul with all the staff, not just me, but eventually I did become singled out because he took to reading things that I had written and he used to red ring them, and he kept saying, 'you're so stupid, you should be neater'. He would actually be so silly; wretched little mistakes, 'how can you do that' and it 'doesn't give a very good impression', it wasn't going out to anyone other than him, and that wounded my self-esteem appallingly, but the top and bottom of it is you're in a relationship there where someone is superior to you, so you take it.

Did you inform them you were dyslexic?

I told them I had a problem, but I didn't tell them it was so bad; I've always been scared of saying it is dyslexia. I do have a problem and under stress, it is worse than what it is. I don't tell people because I'm scared of being called stupid.

Do you anticipate that having dyslexia will give you any difficulties once you've left university?

I want to practise law ... I gained confidence during the course, so I am trying my best to get a degree, so that's going to be proof that I can actually do it. Getting out there and learning the process of being a lawyer is something that you learn while doing the job, and again you have access to things like secretaries and you do have time to look things up. I'm anticipating that there won't be too many problems and hoping that lawyers on the whole are going to be a little more supportive.

Working for a firm of solicitors, would you tell them straight away about your dyslexia or would you leave it until someone identified a mistake?

I'd have to tell them immediately, especially if I was going to ask my department for a reference; they would tell them anyway.

So you've accepted that it's dyslexia and it's going to be a problem.

I've accepted dyslexia and I know it's going to be a problem, but I haven't accepted that it's going to be a problem.

In general, how do you feel at the moment about being dyslexic?

It's all linked in with how I feel about myself and performing and what my capabilities actually are, and it's very difficult to define that in words of one syllable and in simple statements, but I feel very negative about the whole thing generally.

Is there a positive attribute to being dyslexic?

The positive side is possibly I'm more articulate and capable of expressing myself verbally, but that is no substitute for hard qualifications.

Comment

Assessing severity

As has already been discussed in Chapter 2, one of the difficulties in considering dyslexia is in trying to estimate its relative severity. The first problem involved in this is that there may be different subtypes within dyslexia with different cognitive profiles, such that it is not possible simply to place all individuals with dyslexia along one scale. As with visual impairments, there may be a wide variety of impairments that give individuals quite different underlying difficulties and, in turn, quite different challenges on a day-to-day basis. Another problem is that our present techniques for assessing dyslexia are still in the early stages of development, and are still quite crude.

In the past, assessment of children leaned heavily on reading and spelling scores, and only recently have attempts to quantify the processing difficulties underlying these been in evidence, with the use, for example, of phonological (sound-awareness) tests. Past approaches to assessment have been particularly problematic in considering adults, because many adults with dyslexia have overcome their reading difficulties to the extent that they are not revealed by conventional reading tests. Yet another problem particularly marked by adulthood is that it can be difficult to distinguish between primary and secondary factors when assessing someone's performance. Andy commented that he did worse when he was under stress, and, despite the sympathetic context in which the writing task was carried out, several of the students with dyslexia reported that this was a stressful task. So, in this case secondary as well as primary factors may have been impairing their performance.

This is one of the issues at the heart of assessment: in measuring someone's performance, how close are we to measuring their competence? Competence is assumed to be how well someone can perform under ideal conditions, and performance is a measure of how they actually do. Despite these reservations, it was considered that, at a global level, distinctions could be made between those individuals with the most and those with the least severe difficulties in our sample of students with dyslexia. As can be seen, Andy was one of two students to receive the maximum score of 12 on the critical 12 items on the Adult Dyslexia Checklist. Critics have pointed out that as this is a subjective checklist, it may not be a reliable indicator of the objective difficulties of an individual. Even if this is the case, it can be argued that individuals' own perceptions of their difficulties are an important part of any assessment and may have an important role in affecting how well individuals perform on dyslexia-related tasks. Andy commented several times on his low self-esteem and how he felt that his past experiences of learning still had a negative influence on him now. Andy's poor performance on the writing task validates his self-assessment on the Adult Dyslexia Checklist and confirms that he was one of the most severely impaired students in the sample.

Environmental factors

As many in special education and disability research have pointed out, severity alone is not necessarily a good predictor of how someone will fair; the other side of the equation is how far the environment either ameliorates or exacerbates an individual's difficulties. Andy clearly saw his school and, to a lesser extent, his home environment as unsupportive of his difficulties. His experiences at school are strikingly similar to those recounted by the eight adolescent boys with dyslexia interviewed by Edwards (1994). In both cases violence from teachers, unfair treatment, humiliation, inadequate help and teasing were reported as predominant features of school life. This raises the question of whether those who have more severe impairments are at greater risk overall of negative reactions in situations where their underlying difficulties are not recognised or understood. Although parents are often seen as a source of pressure or anxiety in the educational literature, reports by dyslexic individuals and sympathetic clinicians stress the importance of parental support and belief in the child, especially when the school environment is negative.

In a study of successful adults with dyslexia, Scott, Scherman and Phillips (1992) found that all emphasised the support of their parents as critical in helping them to cope successfully with their difficulties. Andy felt that his family were generally unsupportive because they did not understand the nature of his difficulties. This is related to the point he also made about the difficulty of having a hidden 'disability' that is not easily recognised or appreciated by others. As he graphically put it, people would be far more inclined to recognise his difficulties if he had a white stick or a guide dog. This point emphasises the need for people to become better informed about the kind of difficulties encountered by individuals with dyslexia. It also emphasises that simply teaching dyslexic people strategies for improving their performance and developing their coping skills is not enough, and that we should also be looking at ways of making environmental changes, especially in terms of other people's attitudes.

The importance of self-knowledge

Like many individuals with dyslexia, Andy felt that he was seen as lazy and stupid when he was at school and felt that as a consequence he had very low self-esteem, which had continued into his adult life. Like the majority of students in this study, he thought that knowing he was dyslexic was of vital importance in the way that he viewed himself and enabled him to have a much more positive self-image. Despite this, Andy felt that the legacy of the past was still with him and made it difficult for him to develop real confidence in himself. This was confirmed by his very low score on the Culture Free Self-Esteem Inventory. On the other hand, he did indicate that knowing he had dyslexia gave him a 'sense of purpose' for the first time in his life, and with help he was able to develop positive coping strategies rather than the avoidance strategies he had used at school. Although more systematic research is needed, evidence of a clinical nature such as this does suggest that some individuals with dyslexia who are unrecognised and unsupported are likely to develop a sense of learned helplessness, and one of the important aspects of being identified as dyslexic is that it may give people the message that they can learn ways of coping with their difficulties.

Coping strategies and support

Andy was consciously employing a number of impressive strategies that he had worked out for himself to help him cope with his work. Like the majority of students in the sample, he was also dependent on the practical support of someone else to help, especially with tasks like proofreading work. Although generally this appeared to work well it does raise further questions about how people feel about having to ask for help and being dependent on the goodwill of others. It also raises more general questions about the sort of support that students with dyslexia would like to receive. Not surprisingly, views on this were diverse and depended in part on the support that individuals had already received. As Andy pointed out, he had got used to having to cope largely on his own by developing practical strategies, and what he would have liked was the opportunity to meet others with similar difficulties because this was something he had never had the opportunity to do.

For each student the balance between personal and practical support may vary, but it does suggest that both should be available. Andy also commented that he was critical of his own work and that it was 'never good enough'. McLoughlin, Fitzgibbon and Young (1994) suggest that adults with dyslexia often have a distorted perception of what normal standards of skills are in specific areas like literacy, and therefore tend to set themselves unrealistically high standards. They suggest that checking out what others can do may be helpful. Like several of the students in the study, Andy spoke of the difficulty of having to read things two or three times before they made sense. Although, because of the severity of his problems, Andy may well have had more difficulty than usual, it is not uncommon for non-dyslexic students also to complain about having to read more complex materials several times before they can make sense of them. This kind of information should not be offered to dismiss or belittle the difficulties that students with dyslexia encounter, but rather to help them gain a realistic picture of the wide range of competencies displayed by non-dyslexic adults.

Positive and negative aspects of labelling

Another issue, raised by Riddick (1995), is that individuals with dyslexia appear to distinguish between public and private usage of the label. Whereas the overwhelming majority of them are positive about the term as a means of personal understanding, a significant proportion of them are more cautious about using the label in public situations because of their fears of negative reactions from other people. Andy illustrated this point when he explained how he had not used the term 'dyslexia' at work and again had not told other students he was dyslexic for fear of being thought stupid.

Summary

Andy was chosen as an example of a student with severe dyslexia; in addition to this, he had had appalling experiences at school, with no support or understanding of his difficulties. Despite these negative early experiences, it is encouraging that Andy has chosen to go on to higher education and has developed his own coping strategies in a subject area (law) that requires a high degree of literacy. He himself points to the importance of his being offered appropriate support by someone who believed in him and understood the nature of his difficulties. Both Edwards (1994) and Riddick (1996) also found that children, adolescents and parents all pointed to the importance of having at least one significant person who believed in the individual with dyslexia. This appears to be particularly important when the individual has already encountered a range of negative experiences.

Chapter 4
Janet

'Look here, I am not ill, I am not stupid, I just can't spell particularly well and I can't read as fast as other people.'

Janet left school at the age of 16, thinking that she was unable to cope with academic work and was not 'diagnosed' as dyslexic until she was 23. She entered university at the age of 27 and is following a social-science course. She was always well supported by parents and friends and has an average level of self-esteem. Her score on the Adult Dyslexia Checklist is below the average for our sample.

The Interview

Do you think that the experiences you had before coming to university are affecting the way you are coping now, your past experiences at school?

If it was down to school I would never have come. Basically, it was so awful I left at 16. I just got out because I hated it so much. It was just so bad. And the support that they gave, well, to start with, in middle school, my dad, who was very keen on our education, was really aware that there was something not quite right, because I have got an older brother and you could just tell I wasn't making any progress. And he'd heard about dyslexia and he went up and spoke to the headmaster and he wouldn't entertain it. He said it didn't exist. So he got really negative feedback and the only thing he could offer was to send me to a specialist school – and who wants to go to a specialist school really? And the other thing was, you can drop back a year. And there was no way I was going to do that when you've got your friends and the stigma that would have been attached to that. It probably would have done me a lot of good, but I was a determined thing and I wasn't going to drop back. That was the first experience.

What specific kinds of difficulty did you have at school?

I had a great difficulty learning to read – really, really difficult. I hated reading.

At what age could you identify, or did your teachers identify, that you had a problem with reading?

Just right at the beginning. Probably middle school was when I can remember it. I was very aware that I couldn't read and had to go to remedial. That was OK actually, remedial in middle school, that was nice, because you went into your English lesson, you weren't segregated. Where, in high school, they took you out – it was horrible. In middle school you would go to your English lesson, but it was just a few of you so you didn't mind just then. I mean, kids, then you're not so worried, and that was good. The woman there was very, very sympathetic and very helpful and she sort of helped my reading and my dad made me read every single night. I had to read two pages when he got home from work. I was forced to, I got bribed to read. I wouldn't read for pleasure ever, never would read a comic or anything. So that was when I was a very bad speller as well.

You were a bad speller as well; what would you say was the major problem?

Out of the two, probably reading was the first, but I came on in that and I could read perfectly all right – and spelling didn't advance. The spelling is really the bad thing now, atrocious. I had a bit of a bad experience in fifth form with reading again. I was quite hung up about it by this time. Plus, in high school, you got taken out and you used to have to go in assembly and to do spellings, and the sixth-formers were the ones that taught you. I had a really bad experience because there was this girl across the road. When we were kids there was an immediate fall out and we were told not to play with them anymore, and this girl had to teach me spelling and I hated it, and I never put any effort in. I looked at them before I went and I never learnt a thing and I just got more and more resentful. And I did that right the way through high school. But when I was in the fifth form in English literature we had to read out [in class]. And this one particular day, because I am quite worked up about reading, I would read out and I would stutter or I would get so worked up and it was a really weird experience. I thought I was going to suffocate, I was running out of air. And this day the teacher made me read and she didn't stop me, and being in the lower sets you've obviously got people who mucked about. I remember this lad who sat next to me and was just heckling me all the way through it and he was laughing and the more he laughed the worse I got, and she didn't stop me and it was absolutely horrendous and I just remember leaving the lesson and thinking, I am never going again and I went and complained and I was really, really upset about it.

Did that teacher know that you had difficulty?

I don't know actually; she did afterwards.

Did she act upon that; she saw the problems you were having, did she say anything to you afterwards?

I think she actually did because I went and complained to my tutor and said that I wasn't going to English ever again and she sort of said: 'Oh, come on', and I think actually she did say sorry and she made me sit down and read, and I read perfectly OK, so she said: 'You can read, and it's just obvious that you've got a thing about it.' So from that point, that was it. I just hated English. I went and sat right at the back of the class, and I remember I used to shove down in my seat so she couldn't see me and I used to talk to this girl and I never learnt a thing. Then I used to think that was really bad, so I left obviously failing English badly. Then I did it again when I was 21, I did 'O' level and I got an E.

Did any teachers recognise you had dyslexia?

No, none of them said anything at all, nobody offered to test me.

At what age were you assessed?

I think I was 23, maybe 24.

It wasn't picked up at primary school or secondary school?

No, they just wouldn't have anything to do with it, you were just stupid when you couldn't spell.

Did your parents recognise that you had a problem in that area?

Yes, they were really good, they really tried through the education system to do what they could and they were really supportive. My dad particularly went to great lengths; I don't think I would have been anywhere near the standard if it hadn't been for him. And he got frustrated because he could see I got frustrated. I mean at the time he wasn't aware of The Dyslexia Institute or anything, he just couldn't find anything out.

Before you were assessed, what did you think of yourself and why did you think you were having difficulties?

I just thought I was a bit stupid really ...The feedback I got from teachers was, you must be lazy. With spelling it was terrible, they said it was careless, really, really careless and I was just stupid and I didn't put enough effort in asking things.

You were probably in the position where you could see your friends obtaining these qualifications and being in the top groups and maybe you were in the lower groups, you were friends with people in the top group, you're usually friends with people on the same sort of level: how did it affect you?

They were really very nice, the friends that I had. I'm still quite friendly with them. We all lived in the same street and we played out together when we were kids and we grew up through school and I just stayed friendly with them. I made other friends within the group, but we were all quite close, and there was another friend who was in remedial originally. She got out of it in middle school. She had trouble with spelling and her mum thought she might be slightly dyslexic, but they weren't boastful people who were much better than you, they just accepted you for what you were and I accepted them for what they were and it wasn't really an issue.

When you knew you were dyslexic, at the age of 23, did that change the way you saw yourself and did this have an effect on your academic work and relationships?

I thought at least I'm not as stupid as I thought I was. I must admit, it sounds stupid because the career I chose was hairdressing and I did very well in it – but I always thought I could do something better than this, but I didn't know what. And I thought, well, I'm not academic. But once I was tested I thought, I'll give it a go, maybe I'm not going to get anywhere. So I went back and did English language and I got a 'B' and the teacher was brilliant.

The teacher was sympathetic to you?

Very sympathetic.

Did you approach the teacher before you took the lesson?

She was very approachable anyway, and everybody had done terribly and everyone had failed at least once in the class. But she was very, very good. She was one of these people, although she would give you constructive criticism, she would praise you first and she would say, 'Oh this was great', and she would point all the good points out. And she said, 'But we need to look a little bit more on this and a little bit more on that', but she made you positive instead of making you negative, which is what they did at school. She was brilliant. You went away with the assignments and you thought I want to do it well because she is so nice and encouraging. The feedback you got from her was great and she was so supportive. She was the one who told me I could get into university. She was the one who made me have a go.

Did you receive any additional support when you found out you were dyslexic, I presume you went to the Dyslexia Institute, where you had your assessment?

No, not really.

So you didn't receive any additional support there, but you said that your English teacher was supportive?

She was absolutely brilliant at College, she hung around people with problems and I would go up. Because I was paranoid, I really wanted to do well and she was always there to talk about things and go over things and wrote really helpful comments. She always said, 'Don't worry about your spelling. You know it's a problem. I'm not going to come down on you, but do try and make an effort and get a dictionary.' I had never done that before, and because she said it in a sympathetic way I did that. And she suggested that I put in for extra time for the exams this year. I never knew anything about it. So she organised all of that and although there was never any real additional help she was very supportive.

Did you feel that the extra time in examinations helped at all?

Yes I think that was really good with being a slow reader. I can read all right but I am very slow compared with other people. I always find comprehension hard and I really need to read it twice to actually grasp it – and then I can answer the questions, no problem. So that's where I use my extra time, reading more than with the writing.

While you were in post-16, how did you cope with your academic work and did you use any kind of strategies to overcome your difficulties that you had, i.e. your spelling, or were you aware of any techniques that you could use?

Not really. I have got an aunt who was a teacher and I had trouble with the two 'theres' and she wrote some helpful hints down, which she used to teach her children, so I had those. But, really, I've got friends who've been to university and everybody has been really supportive. My dad's a very good speller, so he would check it. And I had two friends and they read all my work over and I would basically write it then readapt it and take it to them and they would check the spelling. If they thought I had written anything that didn't sound too good then they would say how you could write it better and they would help me figure it out. They made me look at it more carefully.

A very supportive background then.

Everybody's brilliant, they've been great.

So, turning to the present, do you think that the sort of problems you face at university are much the same as other students'? What are your specific problems at university, comparing yourself with your friends?

I think probably the same sort of thing – I haven't really discussed it.

How is note-taking in lectures, how do you find that? Because obviously you have a problem with spelling and taking it in.

I can't read some of it. When I read it back it doesn't make sense, especially with words that you're not familiar with. Sometimes the lecturers will actually spell things out, but sometimes I'm a bit frightened – not so much this term, but last term I was very frightened, I felt like I was here by default and that I shouldn't have really been here. What I'm going to do this term is to read other people's notes over that they've made, because I'm aware that I miss words out. I've got a little tape recorder that I take to the lectures, but I find that I don't always have time to listen to them [the tapes] again.

How about seminars, and how are you in speaking in front of a group?

A bit quiet at the moment, I'm kind of sussing people out, I like to feel safe before I start saying anything.

Your experiences at school have led on to university.

I'm like that really, I'm very cautious with people when I don't know them, but I'll speak my mind. Plus, probably, on the education side of it I'm frightened that everybody knows the answer and I don't. I'm still a bit frightened I'll get called stupid – which is daft really, because everybody speaks out and some people get things wrong.

Have you told any tutors about your difficulties at all?

Yes, my head of year he knows, it was by sheer fluke really, because on your form it asks if you have any special needs and I just said to him, 'Do you put dyslexia down?', not knowing really what to do. And he said 'Oh, yes', so I wrote it down. So he knows, and the two people who I've had exams with, they obviously know, because I've had extra time. And my personal tutor knows. And she was very kind and nice and she said that she would ask for extra time for my essays, but I actually refused it because I thought I'm just going to get further and further behind. So I thought it was better to work to the deadlines that everybody else has rather than get so behind.

Are any other of your lecturers aware of that particular problem?

Not all of them.

When you hand an essay in to that lecturer do you say, 'Look I'm dyslexic'?

No I don't.

What's the kind of feedback that you get from your essays?

They've been OK, actually. They've been quite pleased with what I've done, for me. What I aimed was to get to the level of passing everything. This was my personal aim, just to pass everything. I thought get through the first year and get through the first hurdle of actually getting through and take it from there and see what people say. I have been quite pleased. I've had sort of 58s, 60s and 62s.

Do you get support from your LEA?

Yes, I am now.

Are you getting any support in applying for a computer, has anyone come up to you and said, 'This is the kind of software or hardware that you need'?

I actually went to see [the Special Needs Support Officer] in Student Services and she was brilliant. She wrote a letter, she told me to write a letter, she sent my script off and she also told me to price the computers and the software, and she told me what she thought I would need.

You've got the hardware and software allowance. Are you aware there's another allowance as well for buying books and photocopying?

He did say something about this, but I thought that it was all in the same thing and I didn't want to push my luck.

Ideally, what sort of support do you think should be available for dyslexic students at the university?

I'd like help with essay writing, I think that's really where I would like some help, because it has kind of been just guesswork really so far – obviously, you've got a vague idea of what to do. I'd like someone to say, 'Well, look, this is how you can improve it', because when I read my essays back, I thought that some of the English wasn't particularly good. So I am not too sure if it is because I have hit on the points they wanted and I've got the marks for that, because I don't think I have got marks for the presentation and the way it's actually written. I'm sure you get marks for that. Some of the things my friends write, they write it in these posh, fancy, big, long words and it sounds so much better than my work – and I'm thinking, I would like to do that.

Do you tend not to choose those more sophisticated words because of the problem of spelling? Do you think, I would like to use this particular word in a sentence but, well, I'd better not, just in case, because I can't spell it?

I think that it's due to a lack in my vocabulary, because I would look it up if I knew it. You know some words, but you're not desperately sure of them.

When you're looking at a friend's essay you can see a particular word and you think that's a very good word: you can understand what it means, but what's stopping you from actually using that word in your essays?

I don't think about it when I'm writing it, I suppose, and I probably should get a thesaurus sorted and things now. I have got one, I've used it a little bit, and sometimes when I feel I am repeating a word I get my thesaurus out and change it. It's really that, I would like to be able to improve on essay writing, because I think really if you can get your information you should be able to get very good marks for your essays, that's what I think. If you've got the time to do it – as long as you're barking up the right tree.

What aspects of your work do you feel you do well in?

I don't really know. I'm pleased with it. I'm pleased with what I've achieved in my essays, obviously, but really I can't say.

Do you use any particular strategies? You mentioned a few before, strategies that you have found effective in how you deal with your work.

I just basically try and get points and then write something on all of those and look into them, because I think the more points you've got, because I am quite a methodical person, I work through things methodically, so I try and touch on things and make it follow on, that's what I try and do in my essays.

Would you write essay plans to help you?

Yes, definitely. I do essay plans and quite often, with not being desperately confident I quite often go and see the lecturer and say: 'Look this is what I think. Am I on the right lines?' I know they can't give you too much help because it wouldn't be fair on other people.

Do you think that knowing you are dyslexic affects your confidence in your ability to do academic work?

Definitely, you never think you are as good. Now I've been here and got through the first semester, I feel a little bit more confident than what I did last term. But I really thought: 'What am I doing here? I am really not good enough.' And I think I really must be at the bottom of the class because I really am hopeless and I always see myself at the bottom ... I think it probably stems from previous experience at school and it probably leaves a scar.

How do you think your particular personality influences the way you deal with dyslexia, or how has it affected your personality? Can you see a difference between before you were assessed and after? Was there a change?

I think probably, I'd probably be sort of negative towards me and sort of think I'm just no good at anything. That's the sort of attitude. I can get by, but I'm never going to be as good as anybody else, I'll always be slow, and things like that.

Does having dyslexia affect your general self-esteem?

Yes, slightly negative. My boyfriend, he said 'You're so negative about yourself and you're so positive about everyone else and build people up and try to give them confidence, but you, you just don't believe in yourself at all.'

Do you tell other students that you are dyslexic?

A lot of people kind of know, but it doesn't worry me. I think if I had been at school I would have been very cagey about telling people, but now I just couldn't care less what other people think. If they think you're stupid, or if they are being funny about it, then it's their hard luck. I'm too old now to be bothered about what other people think, if they don't like it then it's their problem not mine.

And you have no problems telling lecturers?

If it was necessary I would tell somebody, but I'm not going to worry about it too much. But the people that do know have been brilliant, my friends have been great, especially with writing the essays at first. I mean, every time I handed one in I failed it. I got 58 [%] for my first one and at least I knew something about that one because it was equal opportunities, so I knew quite a bit about it. The next essay we did was very hard. It was a history essay and I couldn't understand the words in the books, I just couldn't understand it, I was tearing my hair out, I was really demented with it, because it was all olde worlde English and I'm not used to reading that, and I really, really found that hard. I was very down on that, and my friends really helped me a lot on that essay, they sort of said, 'Look, tell me what you have interpreted it as.' We really worked together and helped one another, so they have been absolutely brilliant.

How is your short-term memory? Do you have any problems remembering people's names, or figures or numbers?

Numbers I can't remember – telephone numbers I just can't remember.

Comparing yourself with your friends, do you think that is more to do with dyslexia?

I think it probably is, but it's not something that particularly worries me, they just laugh. I remember important things, but in a general conversation I don't remember anything.

Have you ever felt isolated at university because of your dyslexia?

No, not at all.

How about when you were younger, before you knew you were dyslexic?

I got cheesed off and fed up with the treatment and thought I don't want this, it's not helping me with where I want to go. I got a bit annoyed. One of my main things is I felt very frustrated and cheated which has always been there, and I think that's probably why I've ended up getting here and following it through. I have always felt cheated and angry compared with my friends – that I missed out and they got all of these qualifications and they got the jobs that they had and the wages they've been paid. I trained for five years and I got paid nothing compared with them and I worked equally as hard as they did and got very little back. I think that the school really badly let me down, to be honest, and I think that they need to re-look at things. I don't know how they can make things better, I really don't know what they can do, but I think we should be tested. And I think if anybody in classes has sort of behavioural problems or things like that come across, I think people should be tested. If they obviously come across as bright but are useless at their work, I think they should be taken away and tested, to be given that chance.

Did it affect your behaviour in class because you were in the lower groups, did that have an effect on your behaviour, did you play up more often?

No I was never like that, I was very quiet.

Would it help you to meet up with other dyslexic students?

Definitely, I would really like to do that, it would be a big help, people having nightmares about work and things like that and having the same kind of frustrations, I think it would help. I think it would be good, then people would realise that they are not alone and could be supportive and stuff. I have spoken to two people since I have been here. One of the ladies on our course, her son's dyslexic and he's now going through his GCSE course this year and they are really worried because he wants to get into the navy and he's got to get certain results, and the backup they're getting, they're very frustrated with it. So I had a long chat with them and she's really pushing the school to get him assessed. And somebody else I know, her son is 8 and she's just had him diagnosed and he now goes to the Institute and he has lessons and she says that he's coming on brilliantly. He's so intelligent and so bright and he has a very adult conversation.

Have you met anyone in the past or now who has ridiculed your dyslexia?

Nobody now, just when I was at school in English, that was the only time.

How did you cope with the situation?

I was absolutely crushed and really upset, I just didn't want to go back and when I see this particular person now I just cringe when I see him.

Do you think dyslexia will have a bearing on the kind of job you have when leaving university? Do you think it will be a consideration?

Not in the field that I am actually looking to get into at the moment.

Which is…?

Careers guidance, that's where I would like to be; I don't think that would have a bearing.

Do you anticipate that having dyslexia will give you any difficulties once you've left university?

Obviously, writing reports and stuff like that, that will always be a problem, depending if I went the administrative way, that's obviously going to be affected. But at the same time, if I get quite good with a computer that shouldn't be a problem. So as long as I work hard and get to the bottom of this computing business, then, hopefully, it won't be a problem.

In general, how do you feel at the moment about being dyslexic?

Not too worried, because I have had help that I have never had before. I was quite overwhelmed in the first week with people saying, 'You've got to do this'. And this nice lady saying, 'You're going to do this and I'll write you a letter', instead of saying 'Don't be stupid', which is what I expected. And this other guy really nagging me all the time. My tutor was so nice, and I have never had that kind of support ever from education.

So, have you found the university generally supportive and the education authorities also?

Yes, I think it's really good, but I think it would be better if you could meet and have people being more critical of your work, even if there were extra lessons. I mean I could do with extra lessons in English. I know they do this at the dyslexic centre, and I was considering going and it would be nice if there was something like that to go to. I know there are certain things going on, but they clashed with my timetable. I couldn't attend any of them, I think that would be brilliant, it would be really great.

Is there anything else you would like to talk about that I haven't raised?

Just more support and I would like to see that in years to come there isn't a stigma attached to it. I mean, at my age it's fine, but younger people.

Is support more needed in schools than it is at university?

I think if you got support in schools that would be a big help because there are a lot of people at school who have achieved nothing when they should have achieved something. And I think there are a lot of people who should get to here who haven't had that opportunity. And I think that if you had more of a backup as well when you got here and if the public got to know more about it and if it became more of a general thing. I have had somebody turn around and treat me as if I was ill and it's patronising. And I just think, 'Look here, I am not ill, I am not stupid, I just can't spell particularly well and I can't read as fast as other people.' And they keep patting you on your head, 'It's your problem', and they treat you [as though you were] stupid and I wish they wouldn't do that. And if it became more of a norm and a word that everybody was aware of and everybody knew somebody who was dyslexic it would be OK. Attitudes of lecturers and teachers, I've not had any bad feedback but I daresay that there will be people in the university who are ignorant of it.

Comment

The school experience

Like others in our sample, Janet struggled through school in the remedial and lower sets and left when she was 16. She had great difficulties with learning to read, but was helped by her father, who would not let her fail and also by a teacher in her middle years of schooling. She appears to have internalised an image of herself as stupid and incapable, but nevertheless had sufficient faith in herself to try again in later years.

Receiving support

Janet has apparently received a great deal of support from several sources, which she remembers, dwells on and comes back to – her friends, her father, a teacher in middle school, at teacher at further education college, tutors at university, Special Needs Support Officer at university, peers at university.

She is open about her difficulties, and it may be this attitude that summons up support for her. It is also possible that she is a person who remembers and dwells on positive experiences rather than negative ones.

The label

Janet does not appear to have particular difficulties in acknowledging the label and does not see the label itself as conveying negative messages – although towards the end of the interview she does say, 'I have had somebody turn around and treat me as if I was ill and it's patronising.' Generally, when she has used it she has found that the label attracts help and support from a variety of sources. She was identified relatively late compared with most of the students in our sample, and she has found positive results from using the label. It has helped her to feel that she should go on trying to achieve and acquire qualifications that will enable her to develop a more interesting career with better prospects. Had she not been given the label, she says that she would have continued to regard herself as slow and not as good as others. She is very positive that there should be more assessment for pupils in schools who are experiencing such problems, and that everyone should be given a chance to achieve their potential.

Feelings about her dyslexia

Janet states very strongly that she has felt very angry and frustrated by her difficulties, 'I have always felt cheated and angry compared with my friends – I missed out and they got all these qualifications and the jobs they had and the wages they've been paid ... I got paid nothing compared with them and I worked equally as hard as they did and got very little back.' She is angry, firstly, that she has these problems and, secondly, that, given that this was the case, no real help was forthcoming at school. Her anger and frustration have proved to be a spur, driving her on to achieve despite her problems.

Features of adult dyslexia

Janet had great difficulties initially in learning to read, but, despite having overcome these with the help of her father and 'remedial' study, she continues to have spelling and vocabulary problems. She has never read for pleasure and therefore her reading experience and vocabulary are limited. Difficulties in acquiring vocabulary have been identified as a feature of dyslexia and other language-learning difficulties. Yet, despite these difficulties, she understands the conceptual basis of the work she is given and can write an essay that shows her ability to handle the relevant information and arguments. Janet does not seem to have particular difficulties in relation to non-academic aspects of her life. She has always had friends who accepted her for what she was and who did not make an issue of her struggles in school. Unlike Caroline (see chapter 7), Janet is methodical and well organised, and does not have to contend with this additional difficulty. However, she does have difficulties in remembering telephone numbers and things said to her in general conversation.

University experience

Janet acknowledges her problems and seeks solutions to them, which is a great source of strength for her. Urged on by those with whom she has discussed her problems, she has informed tutors and others about her difficulties and has received a great deal of help. She finds aspects of study hard, such as note-taking and writing essays, and understanding texts written in unfamiliar styles, but she perseveres and finds strategies to deal with this, such as seeking help from her friends and tutors, using computers and dictionaries. She acknowledges the need to expand her vocabulary, and discusses the possibility of using a thesaurus; to overcome her problems with note-taking, she uses a tape recorder or borrows others' notes. Overall, she is very 'up-front' in her attitude, possibly because she is a mature student and is more confident that the average school-leaver. Personality and other factors may also be at work.

Support for dyslexic students

Janet considers that she has been very lucky during her time at the university so far, but she would like more help with her written work.

In particular, she mentions help with essay writing and more detailed criticism of her work. 'I think it would be better if you could meet and have people being more critical of your work, even if there were extra lessons.' She is happy to tell people about her 'label', but feels that if she discloses her problem in some way it should be possible that this could be 'traded' for extra support.

Chapter 5
Peter

'The main problem, as I see it, with dyslexia is not the lack of literacy or the inability to recall spelling, it's the psychological damage...'

Peter is a 42-year-old mature student doing a degree in the History of Fine Art. His score on the Adult Dyslexia Checklist suggests that his dyslexia is of intermediate severity. Psychometric tests suggest that his self-esteem is low, but his trait and state anxiety fall within the normal range of variation.

The Interview

Do you think that the experiences you had before coming to university are affecting the way you are coping now? Talk a bit about primary school.

The experiences in primary school have all been sorted out really. Any negative problems have been sorted out in cognitive therapy[1]. I got a grant from the Area Mental Health Trust to have cognitive therapy as a test [case]. I'm a good subject, so I'm told, because I say exactly what I think and I don't go back [on] anything. Really, all those ghosts and all those problems had all been exorcised before I came to university. But I came to the university with the expectation that, although in the literature and [in] everything they sent to me, they said that they would welcome people with learning difficulties with open arms, it would be an uphill struggle still. It is a big difference between the public-relations statements that organisations make and the way the organisations are run. I left school at 15 and I was 39 when I came to this university, so a lot of time had elapsed to maybe sort [myself] out and come to terms and stuff.

Did you have any specific problems at primary school?

At primary school it was just one big waste of time in a way. I do have school reports to back up that things were improving but I couldn't read a *Beano* comic when I left primary school. Some teachers were being very generous in their remarks because when I entered secondary school at the age of 12 I didn't know the words on doors were 'push' and 'pull'. That indicates the depth of the problem.

Did your teachers recognise that you had difficulties?

There's no evidence in primary school. I was put into a so-called 'remedial' class with children who had physical problems as well, not disablement but various problems. So I realised I was in a class of odds and sods, if somebody wanted to describe the class. There was some sensitivity with some of the teachers. This was juxtaposed in my mind, of course, with the lack of sensitivity, so I was able to discern it, but there was a mixed-up band of kids and I can remember three children died, which was a big trauma in the class, because they had medical problems. So half of the kids were just in that remedial stream because they had missed so much of their education because of sickness.

What particular problems did you have at school?

Well, I couldn't read. The '11-plus'[2] is a good example because the '11-plus' was a vital examination at the time. The '11-plus' paper was put in front of me and I couldn't fill any of it out because I couldn't read anything. It was pointed [out] to me that I should write my name on the front page and I got as far as my name and that was it. I couldn't read any of the instructions or any of the questions so I sat in front of the paper for the duration of the exam and handed it back blank, which was a great psychological blow because everybody else in the exam was writing.

Did your parents recognise that you had difficulties at school at all?

Yes, my parents took down everything said by the teachers as wholly correct and never questioned [it].

So you had no formal assessment of dyslexia at school?

No.

Was the school aware of dyslexia as being a learning difficulty?

I never heard the word 'dyslexia' until I was 23 but in secondary school in the second year, at the age of 13, one of the English teachers was getting us to do various tests, which seemed to indicate to me he had some sort of interest. We were taken to the gym and asked to walk down the basketball lines to see if we could walk straight and there were some tests done, so I believe that was some research [being] done into learning difficulties but we weren't told why this was being done and there was speculation as to what it was about, but it highlighted that we were different.

What age did you have an assessment for dyslexia?

At 23.

What made you take that?

I had left school at 15 and went into the family business of painting and decorating, and hated it, and at 23 wanted maybe to train to do something else. [I] applied to the retraining board and they gave me, at [the] Nelson Street Job Centre, an entry test, and I said to the man, 'I'm not going to do very well in this test', and that was the first time I'd ever indicated to anybody outside the immediate family that I had a problem. I sat the test and failed miserably and told the man why. I'd never voiced it to anybody before and he said [that] it wasn't a problem; they'd got a lot of people [like that]. It led to a 10-month remedial course at local college, full time, and my allowance paid me more than my wages as a painter and decorator, so it seemed an attractive thing to do for 10 months. During the first week I was given an inherited IQ test, which came out rather higher than expected and they said [that] I must be dyslexic.

Before you were assessed, what did you think of yourself, and why did you think you were having these difficulties?

When I was a child I thought I had done something dreadfully bad and that I was being punished and [that] there was some god or gods playing with my little life just to torment me. I got quite paranoid.

Did knowing that you were dyslexic change the way you saw yourself, and did this have any effect on your academic work or relationships with other people?

Absolutely, yes. I then thought I could reach the potential I always suspected I had. It always dawned on me that I was rather more intelligent than the other people in the class but I couldn't really make any sense of that. It was a rather confusing situation, but at that age I thought 'Yes! I can', and that 10-month full-time course did change things.

When you had your assessment done, did you receive any additional support or help for your dyslexia?

No. The Institute was run by a few well-meaning helpers. It seemed to me it was rather organised like somebody might organise a church jumble sale, with well-meaning people who tend to do anything, whether it's helping dyslexics or protesting against the hydrogen bomb. It was something for them to do. So I got to see quite a few well-meaning people and I was assessed by someone who was hoping to be a teacher in special needs, but it wasn't an official assessment, but I believed it was this thing dyslexia and that's when I started to hear things like dyslexia was an excuse for middle-class children.

How did you cope with the academic work? What kind of strategies did you use to help you overcome your dyslexia?

I switched off. Either switched off or became disruptive. But disruptive in an intelligent way because I could always spot the teachers and spot what they were interested in. When I say disruptive, I didn't want to upset them or annoy them, I just realised what distracted them, so I soon realised what their hobbies were and their interests, so, to amuse myself, I used to get them on talking about that and often it worked. But class discussions ... I'd enjoyed class discussions and the reports I have said I was well above average, so there was no problem with that. It was just writing it down.

In general, do you feel your family have been supportive or unsupportive?

My mother was very supportive, but my father was very hostile to the whole thing. He was very negative, and he couldn't understand, and was very let down, and there was no support from my father but quite a bit from my mother.

What support did they give you?

Just no more than comfort. They didn't understand there was a problem or what the problem was. The greatest problem was that I appeared to be intelligent, so why did I appear to be intelligent and didn't learn? It was probably lack of application and that's what father thought at the time.

Is any other member of your family dyslexic, or do you suspect dyslexia?

There's only one aunt who had literacy problems, on my mother's side.

Does your sister have any problems?

No. My sister doesn't have any problems. Nobody else appears to have a problem. But that's not unusual for people who go into manual work. They don't need to be that literate so perhaps there was but it was disguised, and I think there is and it is disguised and they have done jobs where they don't have to be literate.

Why did you choose to study at this University?

I sent off for the various prospectuses for universities and colleges to find [out] if there was a degree course in which I would be interested and the History of Visual Arts in the Modern Period was just what I was looking for because I have always been interested in visual arts.

Was dyslexia ever a consideration when you were applying to this institution? Did you think, what are the support services like?

Well, yes, because it said in the booklet that it welcomed people with disabilities.

Turning to the present, do you think that the sort of problems that you face at university are much the same as other students'?

Yes. I think that I have a distinct advantage in the fact that I have had so much experience of life that they can't fob me off with excuses, but apparently, from talking with some full-time students, well, they have real problems.

What specific difficulties are you having at the moment? Let's say, note-taking, assignments, reading, presenting seminars, taking time to complete work?

The course leader is on a sabbatical and we now have another course leader who doesn't know me at all. I have to keep reminding them that I can have an amanuensis at the exams in May and the person keeps telling me that they are very busy, and they are so busy that they don't have time. So taking notes at lectures is a problem. I have a very good portable tape recorder but the problem is transcribing. It is almost impossible for me to transcribe.

How about time taken to complete assignments when you are given work to do? Do you find yourself working harder?

Because they have documentary evidence [of my dyslexia] they have to give me extra time, but other students on the course are really annoyed about this and this has caused a problem, and apparently in the last few weeks there has been a letter written to complain that certain students have been given an unfair advantage because they have been given extra time, and they believe the students given extra time will get a better degree because they have been given longer, but that's because they are retired teachers, from the same ethos of my school days.

Do you have to present seminars and how do you find it?

No problem. I love to be the centre of attention. My job of working in the family firm led to involvement in the trade association, led to working for a lot of bodies within the construction industry, so now I have to give presentations and speeches and doing public relations. Sometimes I am interviewed on radio, so no problems at all.

Reading out aloud from notes?

I don't. I never read from notes. I think about it. I have headings and subheadings with memory joggers but I don't have a transcript. I just do it. I structure it as it's presented. That way it comes over very natural and relaxed and interesting, but the people who are keeping minutes of a meeting [and] who want to see the transcript get very annoyed because there isn't one. That's how I cope.

Essay writing, is that a problem?

It takes a very long time but it's not a problem. There is a reluctance to give extensions. The fact is that someone who is dyslexic can use it as a excuse. I mean they could be lazy as well as being dyslexic, which is my case, so you can use it as an excuse. There is a problem with essay writing but I've overcome it and I've just submitted a dissertation and I have two more essays to complete the course.

Have you told any of your tutors about your difficulties and, if so, what was their response?

Everything from indifference to every other student claims they are dyslexic, and they're fed up of hearing about it. One part-time tutor said to me he is fed up of people asking for extensions because they're dyslexic, they're hard up, they're gay, they're black, they're pregnant, etc. and dyslexia is just another one of the menu of excuses that students think up.

Is there any tutor who has been sympathetic?

There is one who has been sympathetic. The original course leader's son is dyslexic and I thought that was just an excuse, but apparently he [the son] is. He doesn't understand about dyslexia, as most people don't, but some of the tutors now in the final throes of the whole course are now saying to me that they see a distinct difference in my work and [in] people who are claiming to be dyslexic because my spelling is bizarre and not [just] bad. Where other people's is consistently bad, mine is bizarre and they can see a difference, so perhaps they are coming round to it, and they have to, because of the university's policy, because I could actually complain, and if I made an official complaint that tutor could be suspended, and that has happened over something else so that is not the way I would want it to [be]. I would not want them to be motivated because of that. I'd want them to be motivated because they are providing a service to a whole range of students.

Are you currently receiving support for your dyslexia?

Not from the University.

Or from the local education authority?

No. I haven't been allowed extra time for an exam yet even though in the course regulations I am [allowed]. This year I'm going to insist on it because my honours degree is solely dependent on what I do this year, so I am going to insist on it. I am allowed an amanuensis and I have to constantly ask and ask and ask, and I'm not confident that the course leader has done anything about it.

Ideally, what sort of support do you think should be available for dyslexic students?

I think there should be a number of people who have dyslexic students as almost clients and they see them through the whole course of their study. Not hold their hands, but are there as sort of a support worker. People who have the authority to make things happen. Academics aren't good administrators and, because it's unusual, they might not have come across many people. Basically, I don't have any confidence that any of the tutors will do anything they say they are going to do with regard to help with being dyslexic. They all say they understand but nothing happens.

Do you agree there should be a support service to help with essay writing?

There is now in the course that I'm doing two semesters of study skills which would then identify anyone with a problem. So if somebody enrolled ..., [but] the fact is that on a part-time course I think anybody who wants to do it is enrolled regardless of their background, because I think bums on seats are more important than getting people who really want to do it. During the two semesters of learning skills anyone with a specific learning difficulty will be isolated, and the tutor who now organises it, I believe, is sensitive to the whole thing, so [in] this particular course I think there would be some support. Perhaps there have been other students on the course who have been dyslexic. I think there might have been but there has been such a high dropout. Last year three people sat Honours. This year there are nine of us so we are the best year they have ever had. Most people drop out in the first year and it dwindles down, and some of the pupils will have learning difficulties I am sure.

What aspects of your work do you feel you do well in?

Oral presentations, although not marked on my course. Class discussions I excel. That's not assessed, of course. Not officially assessed anyway, and in this last year, the fourth-year exams, dictating the exam answers to an amanuensis I did exceptionally well. I moved from a fail to 70% in some questions.

What strategies have you found effective in helping you deal with your work?

The coping strategy that I have is the fact that if I can't make many notes during the class. I am aware that I might make one page of notes where other people might make 10 or 20 pages of notes. My appreciation of the subject matter is no less than theirs, so while other people write down copious notes it is not always that much help. The fact is that you are making lots and lots of notes, but I am in an arts subject where there is no right answer. Perhaps if you are in a science where there are right and wrong answers the fact that you don't always catch what the lecturer has said in notes could be vital. But in my subject it is not. It's more how it is appreciated. And in written work I do my background reading and I take hand-written notes of anything I think might be useful, with page references, and once I have completed that process I sort those pages into piles. I enter some sort of structure, then I start with whatever I think is the bit that I am most confident with of the essay, and then the essay is padded out from there.

Do you use any form of technology at the moment? Before you mentioned a dicta-phone? Any other forms?

For writing I use a word processor.

How would you cope if you didn't have it to use?

I couldn't. I wouldn't be able to do anything I do. Even if in my job I didn't have a word processor I would have to go back to just doing purely manual work.

Do you think that knowing you are dyslexic affects your confidence in your ability to do academic work?

Yes. It has been for a while, but perhaps it is changing now, but it has been for a while quite fashionable to have something wrong with you. So I mean I came out about it and it's almost like coming out that you're gay, coming out that you're dyslexic. People tend to crowd round and be very interested. Instead of shying away they were rather interested. Now it is quite common and most people have heard of the problem. It devalues this feeling that you're flawed or you are being punished or something. It is a neurological disorder and you just have to make the best of it.

How do you think your particular personality influences the way you deal with dyslexia, or, conversely, has having it had an influence on your personality?

Until about 23 or mid 20s I was very content to be an introvert and very shy, but that's because of lack of confidence. I am naturally an extrovert. People observed there was a change overnight. The fact is that I could see that perhaps it could be turned into an advantage in some cases and that is through having an interest in philosophy; the idea that something that appears to other people to be a weakness might be a strength.

Does having dyslexia affect your general esteem and, if so, in what way?

Yes. As a teenager I had great depression, and became very moody and rebellious, but I don't know if that was part of my personality to do with dyslexia. But I did feel wronged and I did feel persecuted and I did feel that the establishment, whatever that means, had dealt me a very bad deal and I had a chip on my shoulder, which also left me in my 20s. But this feeling of inadequacy, stress and anxiety came over me when I had to do anything in written form and what I now would identify as a panic attack.

Do you still suffer from 'panic attacks'?

No. I don't, because of cognitive therapy, but I now understand how panic attacks work.

At what age did you receive the cognitive therapy?

It was two years ago and that has virtually eliminated it [panic attacks].

Do you tell other students that you are dyslexic?

In a way I do, but I do it in a humorous way. I don't believe now that it is something that you should tell everybody. I believe now that you should only tell somebody if they need to know it.

What sort of reception do you get from the people you tell? Is it generally positive?

It can be all sorts of different reactions. You can tell someone you're dyslexic and 3 days later they tell somebody else you're schizophrenic because they get the terms mixed up. People's awareness is poor and they tend to see it as an excuse for literacy and numeracy problems. Maybe one in five people might say, 'I think I'm dyslexic too because sometimes I have problems spelling words', so there is poor awareness of what it is because it is a term that's so bandied about now. So much so that I have now stopped using the word dyslexia. I now say I have specific learning difficulties.

Do you ever ask students or staff for specific help? For example, proofreading a piece of work.

I haven't. The tutors have told me they are not sure whether it would be in line with the course regulations to proofread any work, and I don't think they want to give any help actually. But with the dissertation I was given quite a bit of help, and I was allowed to submit drafts and spelling errors were pointed out. Nobody helped me with the final copy of the dissertation. I believe it is reasonably well presented but I don't know. I put an extra page in. They said I wasn't allowed to put anything in that mentioned it [dyslexia] but an extra page found its way in that mentioned it.

Are there any situations that you find particularly difficult or embarrassing because of your dyslexia? For example, writing a cheque in public.

Yes, all the time, because people consider me intelligent. So I'm given things to do and people actually ask me for help in filling forms out. I mean forms don't intimidate me, they're not a problem, but I will often find that [people ask me] and then you have the problem of telling people what your problem is. But I get over that now because being registered as disabled I carry a green card and I show them the card, and when I show people the card that says I'm dyslexic somehow it convinces them that it is a legitimate problem.

Any other examples of problems that you might experience at all?

Yes. All the time. I make constant errors with 'yes' and 'no' questions on official forms, and I might send something off to a department and I've ticked the wrong box and it takes an awful lot of explaining why I've said 'yes' when I meant 'no'. I've reversed figures and maybe later on I'll notice the mistake. But when something's done it's put in the post. A typical error nowadays is when people want information quickly and I have to write it down and fax it to them. Once you've faxed it, that's it. So, yes, it is a problem but there don't seem to be any consequences. I've never suffered any bad consequences because of it. It just needs more work.

Have you ever felt isolated at university, or when you were younger, because of your dyslexia?

Absolutely. Perhaps not at university because by the time I had joined this course I was fairly secure anyway, but in my earlier years, yes. As if there was me and everybody else in the world.

Why have things changed at university?

I think things have changed for me anyway because there was a great gap between leaving school and coming to university and I did a course before I came to this university. I had done half of a Certificate [of] Education course, sponsored by a local college because I had done some part-time teaching there and they sponsored me to do it. I have a teaching qualification now which can be extended to a full degree by another year's study, which I'll do in the near future possibly. So, yes, there was, but there isn't now.

Do you know or meet up with other students who are dyslexic at the university?

No.

Would you find it helpful if you could?

No, it wouldn't help me but maybe I'd find it useful in maybe helping others. I think it would be very helpful to share with people, anybody who is older than 20, to share with people in their teens, because they would find that their experience wasn't just unique, that it was typical and that would probably help them a lot. The thing is about a dyslexic person of course, if you come across a dyslexic who's a teenager, they might appear to be quite dull. It's just because they're so withdrawn and shy that their true personality tends to be masked by the problem. So the problem takes over their private life as well as their academic life.

Have you ever met anyone in the past who has ridiculed your dyslexia, and, if so, how did you cope with the situation?

At school lots of teachers ridiculed it constantly. At secondary school I had two periods of French and two periods of German which I had to sit through and those teachers didn't know my problem with English of course. It doubled up and trebled up and quadrupled up because you went to different teachers for different subjects and each teacher tended to ridicule or say things, which would tend to add to it, and I became just numb to it, but particular things do stand out, but they stay in my conscious memory and [are] not relegated to an unconscious mind, which needs something to switch them on. I remember them in the front of my mind and they come to me quite often and I dream about them. I keep dreaming about being back at school and being told that I am lazy, stupid and silly and if I don't learn to read and write I won't be anything. I won't get a job, I'll never learn to drive, I'll probably be on the streets sleeping rough. When I left school I remember walking down the drive from the school and feeling elated at leaving school, as if I'd left prison, looking back and saying 'I'll never enter this place again', but looking forward with great fear about how would I cope in adult life. It was very scary.

Do you anticipate that having dyslexia will give you any difficulties in the future?

Absolutely, it will give me difficulties because I have lectures on this course. I have assignments to submit and there's exams in May, and I've put a proposal to the Department of Historical and Critical studies to do a PhD through the MPhil route. It looks now that I may do it with another university because maybe they are a bit more organised. What I mean is, with this institution I think it will take a year to set up, and with the other university I think I may be able to start this October. However, I will see what happens.

In general, how do you feel at the moment about being dyslexic?

I think at the moment I now see it is not a disadvantage because many other people have things in their lives that have provoked the same problems, emotions and feelings and they've turned them into an advantage. The main problem, as I see it, with dyslexia is not the lack of literacy or the inability to recall spelling, it's the psychological damage, and if you can get over that you can use it to advantage. If you stayed in prison you'd suffer for the rest of your life. So it can be turned into an advantage.

Is there anything I haven't raised that you'd like to talk about?

Yes, the dyslexic problem as I have seen it is not just restricted to academic work or to things like having to fill out a form or to writing a cheque or things like that. It tends to affect your whole life. It affects areas that other people mightn't thing about. It affects relationships and forming relationships, and the difficulty in forming relationships can be a problem. Then you have to develop those skills perhaps 10 years later. So it can [be a problem] and I think it often might ruin someone's entire life, not just, as it's seen, as the difficulty in doing academic work. If the university was wanting to help dyslexic students I think that any counsellors or advisers should be aware of any psychological damage. I mean, if you give someone a word processor and a tape recorder that might necessarily help them, but whether you can give each student the therapy they need, the reconstruction they need, I don't know. The psychological damage stemming from maybe the experiences at school, through frustration caused by being referred to as stupid and lazy despite being a perfectly intelligent person. The problem is that if you have been lazy or if you have done something stupid you can't even cope with that criticism, so constructive criticism is received in a negative way, so therefore you are actually in the prison with the keys on your side.

Comment

Peter's dyslexic experiences are perhaps typical for mature people whose primary and secondary education took place during those years when dyslexia was not a recognised condition and when everyone, including himself, was confused by the discrepancy between his intelligence and his poor school performance. In common with other dyslexics' experiences, this confusion produced different attitudes in different people: his mother was supportive, his father hostile. At primary school there seems to have been a recognition that something was wrong, with the result that he was put into a class with children with a range of different problems, including, apparently, terminal illnesses. One can only speculate how traumatic all these children found being segregated into the same special group. At secondary school the problem seems to have been attributed to a combination of stupidity and laziness, with the now-familiar tales of being subjected to ridicule. At university the general hostility seems to have persisted, albeit for different reasons. Some of his peers are hostile because they see him as being given unfair concessions, an attitude which is, regrettably, also found in his tutors, who resist giving him the concessions to which he is entitled. Whereas in school he was probably seen as a malingerer, he is now seen as a manipulator, an attitude which may be fostered by the more enlightened equal-opportunity policies of the last few years. It seems he just cannot win.

Peter's own attitudes are similar to others reported in this book. For example, the early bewilderment ('some god or gods playing with my little life just to torment me'), deriving from the contradiction between his profound disability (being unable to read 'push' and 'pull' on doors), and the deep conviction that he was intelligent. It's difficult to know whether his decision to leave school and go into the family business would have been different if he had not been dyslexic. The turning point seems to have been the recognition by an enlightened civil servant at the job centre that he had a specific problem. His subsequent diagnosis changed his attitude to his dyslexia and, consequently, his life. Before this he reports being shy, introverted, moody and rebellious, with what he now recognises to have been panic attacks. Diagnosis led to an overnight change in his perception of himself. This was recognised by others, not just himself. The pioneering referral for cognitive therapy built on this change, helping him to come to terms with his disability ('all those ghosts and all those problems had all been exorcised before I came to university').

Peter's final remarks provide, possibly, one of the best summaries of the dyslexic experience. It alerts us to the fact that there are really two problems. The first is the actual disability – the problems with reading and spelling and the educational difficulties these cause. The second is the constellation of psychological problems that result from these difficulties – the damage to the individual's development and his/her relationships with others. This is also evident in many of the other interviews.

Notes

1. Cognitive therapy is a form of psychotherapy, the goal of which is to encourage clients to restructure their perceptions of themselves and of the world. This strategy is based on the assumption that the clients' current perceptions are inappropriate and are therefore a significant, but not complete, cause of their problem.

2. This was an ability test used to select children for grammar school, administered when they were about 11 years old. It was discontinued when grammar and secondary schools were replaced by non-selecting comprehensive schools in the late 1960s and early 1970s.

Chapter 6
June

'I would often cry and want to run out of the class because it was just too painful. They just laughed, even the teachers laughed.'

June was a 41-year-old student who was taking an access course in preparation for taking a degree course. Like several of the students in this study, she commented that volunteering to be part of the study was for her part of the process of coming to terms with her difficulties. She found talking about some of her past experiences a painful and upsetting thing to do, but was emphatic that she wanted to carry on. On the Battle Culture Free Self-Esteem Inventory, June's score indicated that she had low self-esteem. Her score for state (present) anxiety was low and her trait anxiety score was average. She received a relatively high spelling-error score on the free-writing task, which fitted closely with her own account of her difficulties.

The Interview

Do you think that the experiences that you had before coming to university are affecting the way you are coping now?

The experiences I had at school were so dramatic, because when I went to school dyslexia was not even heard of; if it was I certainly had never heard of it, and the teachers punished me, not just giving me lines and keeping me in [after school], but physically punishing me for mistakes that I did not understand. I simply couldn't see them and I knew that I was different from other children, but I got more and more smacked and more and more punished and humiliated, so that I actually withdrew into myself and become so ashamed that by the age of 8 I'd withdrawn so much that I was frightened of other people finding out that I had an English problem, and I really went into a world of my own. I didn't have friends, I was too ashamed, and that stayed with me until a few years ago, and still it can have an effect unless I particularly bond with somebody straight away and get on with them and I'm open and honest with them, then it's all right; but with some people you cannot gel with straight away you do stand back a little bit and people then think that you're reserved and shy, but you're not, you observe and assess people before you ever tell anybody.

So what kind of specific difficulties did you have a primary school?

It was everything to do with English. I couldn't read, I couln't spell, I could look at a book and it was just letters. I didn't know what they said, so from a young age I just looked at the pictures and made up stories. I found that my hearing become my number one thing. If the teacher read a story I learnt it pretty quickly; I remembered it and that stayed with me, but I couldn't write it at all until I was 11.

How about the problems at secondary school?

By that time I was alone, I never got any help, everything I learnt was by myself. By the time I went to secondary school I was just accepted and tolerated, this person is thick and stupid but, because she was a pleasant person and never disrupted the class but worked hard, they never bothered. I was still humiliated, especially if I had to read out in class, I would often cry and want to run out of the class because it was just too painful. They just laughed, even the teachers laughed.

Did the teachers recognise that you had any difficulties?

Of course they knew I had problems, but they ignored it, nobody came up to me and asked why. If anyone asked me the question verbally I could answer them, but I simply couldn't put it down on paper, I was so nervous in English. And I know that some of the blindness to words was due to nerves at that particular age and it still really hurts today. I mean really hurts.

Did your parents recognise that you had difficulties?

They were told when I was 6 that I must be a great disappointment to them by the school I was at, that I would never achieve great things, [that] I was thick and stupid. My parents never bothered and they accepted that, they weren't educated people. If the teachers said that, that remained true to them, and I was never helped at home or given any encouragement or anything. My parents were practical people and that was it. I excelled at sport, no one would compete

against me. I competed against lads or girls because I went to a small
school and we played a lot of sports together. But a lot of aggression
would come out. They couldn't compete, I was a natural. They
classed me a nice pleasant person, but who was thick and that was it.
There was no help at all. I withdrew; I was not a happy person. I
didn't enjoy school, partly because I could not do a lot of the work
and partly because at the age of 8 I had distanced myself from
people, because I was too ashamed. I isolated myself from the experience I had; it was the only way I could cope with it. My brothers and
sisters who come after had no problem. Some of my father's brothers
and sisters couldn't read or write, whether they were dyslexic or
because of their education, who knows. There is no one else in the
family who has got a problem.

Were you formally assessed as dyslexic, and at what age?

After I left school I went to a pre-nursing college and within the first
4 weeks at college they could not understand, my standard of English
was so poor, they didn't know how I got through school, and I was
assessed by an educational psychologist. I don't know the full extent
of that report, it came back that I was [of] above-average intelligence
and through that I got half an hour a week with this teacher, who
used to try and teach me English. It had no effect, I still didn't understand, I couldn't see it. He was teaching me English in the way it had
been taught through school. I still couldn't see it, if you had two similar words and to me phonetically they sounded the same, that's the
way it was. I did try and face it, we had a good a relationship; that
was the first time in my entire life that I had had any help. It wasn't
until I went into the forces, I wanted to be a nurse and from the age
of 16 I wanted to go in to the forces. I sat the forces exam, and it was
one of the easiest exams I had ever done in my life; it was multiple
choice, there was no writing. I could read the question and had a
time limit, and got what was accepted and went to my interviews. I
come over verbally OK, and then when I went to my 6-week basic
training, again there was no English. It was the same type of questions; yes, we did many subjects, but all answers were multiple
choice, a, b, or c. I excelled in those exams. No writing and no time
limit, although I was most probably one of the last ones in the class to
leave, but I was getting 95 or 98% in every exam, and I had never got
those marks in my entire life. I was shocked, I couldn't understand it.
It wasn't until I started my nursing training; in the first 6 weeks you
go into what they call 'blocks', it's like a school and you learn the

basics, and when I started doing essays that's when (I couldn't even spell 'child care' or anything, even though I had done the certificate) they started querying; they couldn't understand how I got accepted into the forces. I mean I couldn't spell, they sent me to hearing tests, eye tests, and all the physical tests; they found that I needed glasses, which I didn't know, because my eyes were sensitive to light and actually that did help a little bit. That did help a little bit because I found that the white paper was reflecting in my eyes and I could see the letters better. But apart from that my hearing was fine, and this lady came up from Bath, and that was the first time I heard the word 'dyslexia' and she gave me physical tests of balance, she told me that my brain is equal power, I haven't got a dominant side. She asked me if I do certain things left or right handed, and I said, 'Yes, I do'; to me this was normal, and I had to go down there for a weekend and they did some tests. Some of them were IQ tests, all different things and they said I was dyslexic.

Before this assessment, what did you think of yourself and why did you think you were having these difficulties?

I thought I really was thick and stupid, I was so young, only 16 years old.

Did knowing that you were dyslexic affect the way you saw yourself?

No, not really, I hadn't really had it explained to me. They told me that if I wanted to have lessons I would have to pay for them, and I couldn't afford it, so nothing was done. But I had this certificate and the tutor at the nursing [college] used to take me for half an hour a week and try and get me to recognise my spelling mistakes.

How did you think about yourself?

It was just the same, they hadn't really explained to me what dyslexia actually was, so I wasn't sure, all I knew was that I was dyslexic; I was born with it and that's all I knew for a long time. I didn't know that it could be a blindness, it didn't connect in my brain, it went into my brain and I couldn't get it out. Knowing I was dyslexic didn't affect me until 10 years later, when dyslexia started coming on the TV, and people then started to explain what it was or little avenues of what it was. And by then my children were coming along, then I started to come to terms with it because as my children grew up, they were very academic, at the age of 6 they could read better than me, they could spell better than me and they couldn't understand why their mum couldn't do it, so I told them that I was dyslexic. In a way, that was a relief, and I started to come to terms with it.

While you were in post-16 education, how did you cope with academic work?

If I'm working alone I'm OK, but when I'm in class, if I try to write and listen at the same time, the jigsaw doesn't come together; I have big gaps and then I get frustrated, because I have to somehow in my head have all the pieces fit so I understand, and if I don't understand it gives me great frustration, because I'm a slow reader and sometimes, because what I read, it doesn't go in what it's saying because you're concentrating on the word. It takes me a long time to read and read before it can connect, it seems to have to take a hundred times longer if I don't understand sometimes to try and read and find out, to get it connected. I have to think it through logically, I have to see it as a jigsaw puzzle altogether before it suddenly clicks and then I think, 'Oh God that was simple', but it's not and that's when the frustration comes in, because you feel that many people in the class connect these things straight away, and you get angry because you know the answers and you know you can do it, it's just the gaps.

Are any of your children dyslexic?

I think my younger son is. The school says not, but he cannot spell and his handwriting is atrocious, but he knows the answer verbally.

How do you cope with that?

Angry and frustrated because I feel that he is going to suffer the same way as me. He goes to remedial English and he is coming on in leaps and bounds but his handwriting is so bad. At the moment he is taking his GCSEs; his moderator is not going to be able to read his work. [I am] angry and frustrated that he is going to have to go through the same procedure. And I want to get it sorted out now. But I haven't got the money to do that. And I've been pushing the school since he was 6 to get him assessed; they say he is not dyslexic, but I can see the signs, I've been there. We've moved around a lot, so he has not been through one entire education system and that is a problem with him.

Do you think that the problems you face at university are the same as other students'?

No, I face a lot of different problems. I have to be dedicated, I have to work twice as hard, when you actually see them and they talk, research and complete an essay [with no problem]. I have to take twice as long to do my reading and find the information and then I have to try to fit it together like a jigsaw, and then I've got to get it on paper, and, I'll be honest, without a computer I'm lost. I couldn't do without it, because I write as if I'm speaking it, and of course that's not proper English or grammar, and I don't see my mistakes, unless the computer pulls it up, and even then I find it difficult to recognise the correct word. And that's the frustration.

Do you find talking in class difficult?

No, I excel [at it], I'm one of the best, because I can express myself and I'm confident; I'm not frightened to speak in public, I'll answer any question honestly. I use to wear a lot of hats to hide it [dyslexia], but today, because I'm coming to terms with it, yes it's still painful when I think about the past, but I just want to be me, I don't want to wear any hats, I just want to be June, and I want people to accept me as I am.

Are there any other problems that you face?

Yes, the lack of understanding from tutors; they don't understand and I think, if they are teaching and dyslexia is widespread, that they have be told to recognise it and to be able to deal with it. That is the frustration; there I am in college and my English teachers turn round say that they've never taught anyone who is dyslexic. I find that difficult to believe and they don't know how to mark my work and they don't know what they're dealing with.

Have you informed your tutors about your dyslexia?

I put it on my forms. My psychology and sociology tutors said they'll be able to adapt to that. But it's the college system itself, it let me down; I was promised these things and they didn't appear until the very end, so that there were massive gaps from the beginning and I've had to work very hard to catch up, [and] that's not fair. I don't feel I've had an equal chance this year.

Are you currently receiving support for your dyslexia?

Yes. Having a one-to-one with certain teachers and certain subjects and trying to learn at my own pace. If they go too fast in class, I need a good tape recorder so I can keep up, and so I can then go to the library and listen to it and actually make notes to fill in the gaps that are missing [sic], so I actually understand. But I need help in a library, that's the difficult thing, trying to find the information; you don't know which books to go for and that is one of my big problems. There are all these books on a particular subject, you'll look at the index but you don't know which bits you want. That is a problem.

Ideally, what kind of support should be given to dyslexic students?

They need people to talk to and understand, they need to mix with other dyslexic people, so they don't feel alone. It's very important, because we can all help each other and I think that the tutors should make more time for that particular student, they need extra time. Even to go over notes, so that you can go at your own pace. One-to-one tutoring. Also help in finding information in the library, if your nerves get the better of you and you get angry, which I do, because you're frustrated. You know what you're looking for but you can't find it, you don't know how to find it, you need help. Sometimes some of the texts are written in such a way, because you have difficulty interlinking the words, [that] you don't understand what it is saying.

What aspects of your work do you do well in?

I can excel [at] mixing with people. I seem to get on with people like me, but maybe because I've dropped all my hats, I just got my June hat on, so people accept me as I am, and perhaps I'm too open and honest; this can sometimes frighten people. I'm not frightened anymore, I've just got to be myself. In my written work ... no not all! I've actually enjoyed doing English, it has helped me to look at English in a different way, but there is still the pain and frustration there. You can't do what the other students do. They can just sit down in an exam and write an essay and get good marks. For me, even just the punctuation is a task.

What kind of strategies have you found effective in helping you deal with your work?

I have to get out of my head first what's in there. I have to get the information on the computer; if it doesn't ring true then I know I've got gaps missing [sic] and find the gaps and put it in. Thank God for the computer, because you can jiggle it all around until I think the structure looks right; then the tears and the anger and the pain start, when I try to find my spelling mistakes.

Do you use any other techniques, like memory aids?

I find that hard; I can't picture things in my head; I can't see it and that has been one of the angers, this year.

You mentioned before that you are using a computer; how is that helping you?

It's opening the world up for me; before when you [i.e. June] used to write, because I've got terrible handwriting, you couldn't read what you'd written, so you rely on your memory of what you have written, and that might not be what I had necessarily meant. And so that's frustrating, and even if somebody else writes the word for you, you still can't understand their handwriting unless they print it. So that's why the computer is so good for me, because it's actually printed letters, it doesn't matter whether they are capitals or lower case, and I can read them. Once it's printed I can begin to read it and under-stand it. I can't see it in my handwriting nor anyone else's if it's joined up; unless it's printed I just don't recognise any of it, it's frustrating. I feel that my processing in my brain is so fast, and I write fast once I do understand something and I know which way I'm heading, I can excel. Perhaps I have faster brain processing than other, most other people and I've always known that I can quickly come up with answers at the right level, but reading it back is terrible.

How does your particular personality helps you deal with your dyslexia?

Because today I've dealt with so many aspects of June, I've got rid of all these 'hats', and I'm working very hard to come to terms with my problem, I'm trying to keep it in proportion even though there is still a lot of pain there, and because my personality has changed from an introvert to an extrovert and I'm more honest. I'm actually more confident, but I know my limitations. People have more confidence in me than I have in myself at times, but I know I will go on and come to terms with it. I'm more honest with people because more and more people know and understand what dyslexia is; it's no longer this taboo or foreign word. Things are improving.

Does dyslexia affect your general self-esteem?

It can, when you relay the past I can get very upset, but I'm glad I got upset today, because I didn't get upset as a child. It's part of my growth: by crying or getting angry I'm letting it out today. Once I got over that crying or anger then I'm capable of going further. In a way by this interview alone I'm laying some of the past to rest, so I'm going on, but the pain has to come out. I know that you may feel that this [interview] should be stopped, but it shouldn't be stopped, it has to come out and it is good that it is coming out. I'm glad that I can let one of those hats of June go. Some people don't like that and say I shouldn't cry, but it's good I do [so] today.

Do you tell other students you're dyslexic?

Yes.

What kind of reception do you get?

Most of them don't understand. I get asked questions: Why do you have a reader? Why do you have someone who writes? When I explain that I have a blindness but the information goes in all right, but I can't get that information out, that I can't see it and that what I write on a page I can't read, they can't understand [that] because they are just listening to me verbally. They see generally a very motivated and positive person who can verbally put herself over very clearly, [so] they don't understand; and if you meet someone they accept you for who you are, but as soon as they see your written work, it's like horror and shock on their face; they don't associate that side with the side they see of June.

Do you ever ask other students or staff for specific help?

Yes.

Do you find that embarrassing?

I don't find it embarrassing today, I ask anyone for help if I need it. I just feel more angry and frustrated that a lot of the time it is such a process, that you've got to wait weeks and weeks for the help, and they don't understand when you ask for that help. And you feel a burden if you ask someone to do that, because you're so used to your experience at school and you didn't get the help. You eventually become self-reliant, possibly too much so.

Are there any situations that you find awkward or embarrassing because of your dyslexia? Talk about experiences in everyday life, away from academia.

If you're at work and you suddenly get the boss come up to you with these three pages of A4 paper, and he says read this and provide me with comments in 15 minutes. That is when the fear comes in, you actually can't read the paper because the nerves and the fears come in, and you have got to calm down. If I have to give my comments verbally that's fine, but if I have to write, well forget it. You may take phone messages for people; you get some ignorant person comes back and makes fun of the way you have spelt things. I can retain the information well. I can't remember people's names because I can't see names or pictures in my head. I'm able to remember everything they say and I can remember what they look like; if I met them 10 years hence I could remember the conversation, but I can't remember their names.

Have you ever felt isolated at university / college?

Yes.

Would a support service help?

Oh God, yes, you have to be able to talk [to meet other dyslexic students], to be given encouragement and, even if you're in the same room, despite doing different subjects, you can help each other and you're not relying on tutors and things, because you can use so much of their time up on you alone, [and] they will soon get fed up. You need a unit where there will be somebody to help you, who is qualified to teach someone who is dyslexic, even though you go to your lectures and you've got all your tapes and notes, you can sit down with that person and they can help you amalgamate it all together. You need those skills, I know that each dyslexic is a different person and they have different problems, but you need someone there who can understand, because I know you've got to be taught in a totally different way.

Do you know any dyslexic students?

No.

Would you like to meet up with other dyslexic students then?

Yes, I think that it would be very important. Otherwise you do feel alienated. You find that because you are working so much alone, because you have to work in a particular way, different from them; you can't really join in their study or their piece of work because you have to work differently, so you are alienated.

Have you ever met anyone in the past or now who has ridiculed your dyslexia, and, if so, how did you cope?

Yes, every day. At work, I'm honest about it and just say I've got a word blindness. If I said that I was dyslexic, I've learnt over the years, they simply don't know what I'm on about. But if I say I have a word blindness they accept that, but because in many ways I excel in the sense that I'm hard-working and honest and I've always got into a position of authority, I'm reliable, I never break people's confidence, I don't tittle tattle, I'm a very hard worker and I give 200% to whatever I do, then you find people respect you and generally they accept your dyslexia as well; but it is when you get people who really [?], without thinking, they may ridicule your spelling. And you say I have a word blindness, you feel that it has held me back, because I know I'm capable of doing higher jobs than have done [in the past]. I know that when I'm applying for jobs that dyslexia is holding me back.

Do you think your dyslexia will have any bearing on the type of job you do when you leave university?

Yes. It will. I will have to have a job where there is not much [written] English; that's why I've always worked with people, because I can give so much, and most of it is verbal. I can organise anything and take it from scratch and develop good systems. I'm very efficient and I get on with everybody. Two years ago I moved into the area and set up a residents' association and at the time I set it up from scratch and it is still running today.

Do you suspect that having dyslexia will give you difficulties once you have left university?

Oh yes. I'll have it for the rest of my life. I accept that, it's bound to [give me difficulties] but that's why you've got to choose your career so wisely. If you've got a portable computer and you can take it round everywhere it can be helpful, but who knows? Especially since they have this new speech recognition [software], the world will open up. My answer may be different in 5 years' time if I have a speech computer.

In general how do you feel at the moment about being dyslexic?

Frustrated and angry in some ways. I still feel that I have not reached my full potential. I haven't found my avenue of learning yet; I think once I do that there will be no holding me back because I've the determination and I work very hard. Once I hit that avenue I'm supposed to be in then I'll excel and leave everyone else behind. Which I can do if I get on the right line.

Is there anything I haven't raised that you'd like to raise?

I think that each child as they go through their education should be assessed. Not for IQ but for [dyslexia], and then there should be the special help. The younger they can start on this problem, if they've got a problem, the more confidence the [child will have], and the child will not be held back. They will not have to suffer what I've been through. I mean I always wanted to be a doctor, but I was told that I was thick and stupid, and the teachers just said 'you can't be a doctor', but I know damn well that I would have made a good doctor. But that's the way things go; that's the frustrating part. Especially since I've worked with doctors and I know that I can do that just as well; verbally I know the answers. I know that I have a lot more talent than a lot of other people. But I can't 'zoom' in on it, because I haven't been shown how to 'zoom' in the right direction.

Perhaps at university you'll come on in leaps and bounds?

Yes, if the help is there!

Comment

June, like Andy, has very negative recollections of school and reiterates many of the experiences that Edwards (1994) recounted from the eight teenage boys that she interviewed, including physical violence and humiliation in early primary school. One of the difficulties in assessing the impact of dyslexia in adulthood is the degree to which past experiences still play a part in how a person perceives and responds to their difficulties. June points out that she still finds her past experiences upsetting to recall, but also argues that for her this is part of the process of moving on. In talking about her personal qualities of persistence and hard work, June displays those characteristics that researchers have found to be an important component of success in adult life for individuals with dyslexia. Despite June's positive coping strategies and willingness to ask for help, she speaks repeatedly of feeling angry and frustrated by her difficulties. As with the majority of students in this study, June stresses that she has to work twice as hard as other students, especially to produce written assignments. This does raise more general issues of motivation and being able to come to terms with having to work harder than other students to achieve the same results. Unlike those students in the study who found being told they were dyslexic of immediate and considerable benefit, June felt that it was some time before she really understood and benefited from thinking of herself as dyslexic. This may have been because she was initially told at a time when there was far less information and public understanding of dyslexia, and because she was not supported by her family, who in both childhood and adolescence often have an important role to play in explaining what dyslexia means. Interestingly, June sees herself as having fully faced up to her difficulties only when motivated by the experience of her own children's growing literacy.

Chapter 7
Caroline

'The complete lack of organisation is to do with dyslexia.'

Caroline entered university straight from school, and is following an education course, training to be a teacher. She scores quite highly on the Adult Dyslexia Checklist, indicating that she perceives herself as experiencing many problems in everyday life. She has suffered by comparing herself with her sister, using negative coping strategies, and she has very low self-esteem.

The Interview

My parents are both teachers. My mum, from the day I was born, said I was dyslexic. She was saying I was hyperactive as a child and I had a lot of problems and when I went to primary school she kept saying I was dyslexic. I was tested when I was about 10 at my primary school. They would say point to your left hand – and I was getting it right all the way through. She said that I can't be dyslexic then, as if it were [that] I thought my hands were the wrong way round. They didn't believe my mum; they thought she was totally mad.

The teachers did not believe my mum, so she took me to St Bartholomew's [Hospital] to get me tested, and they said I was dyslexic. At about 11 I went to secondary school ... I did my 11-plus [school entrance examination] and then went to a high school. There I was put into a help group to teach me to spell words like 'cat' and 'dog' and words by that time I could already spell. It was completely useless, because people there couldn't read, write or do anything. They told me I was thick, so I sat down and taught myself to read by reading *The Hobbit* at 7, and I couldn't read a word of it, and I can't remember anything about it. It was because my sister did a degree, so she was spot on, and there's me just getting by. All throughout school I hated it – I hated English, I didn't do any English work for 2 years and they never noticed it.

This was when you were in secondary school?

Yes that's right.

And you had your assessment of dyslexia at the age of 10?

Yes, that's right.

And that came out as a positive indicator of dyslexia?

They did test me for GCSEs; I passed the test because I [had] taught myself to read because I had this system where I said, 'I am not going to be stupid.' I did my GCSEs with no extra time, and no help. I got five 'C's and three 'D's. I did English Literature, English Language and Home Economics, which were my three 'D's, then I did Sociology, Maths, Physics, Chemistry, which were all grade 'C's; I didn't particularly try hard at them, but I did really well.

I did my English course work in a weekend perhaps why I got two D's, but I'm not particularly brilliant at spelling, there are people who are worse than me who aren't dyslexic it made me believe I wasn't dyslexic for a time. I went to college and did a BTec and got through that all right, it was a very 'dossy' college and I never did any work and it all came together at the last minute and I just scraped through, then.

So nobody in your secondary school recognised you had dyslexia right until your GCSEs?

I was tested. No I don't think they really noticed. Because I hadn't made it to grammar school I was the top of the school, so I didn't have anywhere as severe problems as people lower down in the school. It was all sort of overlooked; I wasn't a big problem, I could read and write.

What specific kinds of difficulty did you have at secondary school? Was it reading or writing?

I didn't have any problems with reading. I wasn't very good at comprehension. I wasn't very confident writing what I meant, because I'd write what I thought I meant and people would read it and say, 'this is terrible and useless', and I'd think, how? I just switched off, and thought if I could get away with not doing it, I wouldn't do it.

So would you avoid reading out in class in secondary school?

I think I read out aloud in class once or maybe twice; I remember the stuttering and thinking, 'if I ever get asked to do this again I'm not going to'. I still get like that. I'd never do that now.

Did your parents recognise you had difficulties – obviously they did. It must have been very frustrating battling with the schools?

What was interesting was the fact that my mum spotted it and until this year I thought my mum was dyslexic because it was like, 'Oh, you're dyslexic as well'. But I never found out until this year that my dad is severely dyslexic. I never noticed it at all. He is an academic and yet his life is a complete shambles. He's just sort of left things to her [his wife].

Are there any other relatives in the family who have dyslexia?

I think my granddad was on my mother's side. I don't know much about my dad's side. My mum had problems with spelling. She can read books and she can talk through what she means a lot better than she can write it.

In general, do you feel that your family have been supportive or unsupportive to you in dealing with your dyslexia?

My mum was very supportive about the fact that I was dyslexic, but they didn't ever tell me what it was outside academia – so I still felt I was completely useless at things. It was never really instilled in me that it was not my fault. I think they wanted me to keep trying, and if it was my fault I was more likely to try. I don't know, I think they were supportive.

And was your sister very supportive?

She wasn't at all; she made me think, 'I hate you so much that you are so clever.'

What reasons did your teachers in your secondary school give for the problems you were having: were you ever accused of being lazy or stupid?

I think I was accused of being stupid, not so much by my teachers, but my sister [who was at the grammar school] continually telling me that I was thick and stupid. At school I was getting picked on for being clever or posh, but I was never at the top at school but I was always seen as being in the top stream, so it was a bit different, and I remember coming home and meeting my sister's friends and it was like 'She's useless, but there's nothing you can do about it.'

Before you were assessed — were you aware there was a problem then, before?

I remember my mum got accused of abusing me at home, for not looking after me properly, because I was always a complete mess. I was constantly told off for being a mess, being late, losing things. My mum said she had a 10-minute gap in the morning where I would lose my bag or lose my lunch, and at school I would always be 10 minutes late.

Did you receive any additional support for your dyslexia? Did you go to any dyslexia institutes at all?

No, at school I was called 'stupid' and dyslexia was not recognised. At college it was all course work and practicals. Last year they gave me this woman who was really helpful and gave me loads of tips on how to plan and to use colours and use big flow charts for stuff, but it was not really support.

So while you are in post-16 education, how did you cope with the academic work?

I did a BTec [vocational course] that was more practically based. I failed biology.

That was a conscious decision to do a BTec: you were aware of your dyslexia?

My dad said that I'll never pass 'A' levels; my dad said 'do a BTec because you have more chance of getting somewhere', and my mum was convinced that I wouldn't get anywhere.

So when you entered further education, did any lecturers identify any problems?

A teacher looked at my work and said it was useless basically – it was an English essay as well. English – I just can't do it, I just refuse to do it. So I was sent to the specific learning difficulties woman who looked at me and said I was dyslexic. Suddenly someone believed me – and I still wasn't actually told what dyslexia was until I came to university. Because of my teacher-training course I got a lesson about dyslexia. This woman had a dyslexic daughter and was telling us about what it meant to be dyslexic. She was coming up with all sorts of things about your social life, your upbringing, all things that aren't academic. And I walked out of this lecture and suddenly thought, 'Bloody hell, I am dyslexic'. All things that everyone said like 'You can't read' or 'You can't write properly' – I've conquered those in a sense in time. But the way that I do everything, the complete lack of organisation, is to do with dyslexia – that no one ever told me. My mum knew a lot about it, and just expected me to know. It was like 'it's you that's got the problem; you know all about it'.

What sort of strategies have you used to help you cope with your dyslexia? You mentioned earlier something about colour coding technique, did this help at all?

I got taught to plan. I couldn't do it. I can't plan at all. My strategy was to avoid doing anything. I got away with physics, where everyone else would write and I could go and talk to the bloke who was teaching physics and I would chat away to him and explain what I meant again. Then it came to the exam and I felt I didn't do too well in the exam, but I'd always get out of my writing by going to talk to people – my strategy to avoid work.

Do you think that the sort of problems that you face at university are much the same as other students'? What are the specific problems you face?

Essay writing, I'm a terrible judge, I put paragraphs in and I move them about, then I forget which bit is to go into which paragraph, or I start writing a paragraph which is totally irrelevant to somewhere else.

So do your essays sometimes go off at tangents?

Yes. Everyone else seems to be able to write an essay in a day, but I sit down and start writing it and the shortest I think I've written one was from about 9.00 until 7.00, and I didn't have a break all day, I just kept going and going. Eventually I got there, but I still wasn't convinced, I had to get people to check that it did make sense and that it was hitting the criteria.

How about seminars: is there a particular problem that is caused by dyslexia?

I'm all right at talking, but doing a seminar, I can read it, I can't remember it or I won't remember it in the right order. I'm getting better at it, someone said to me photocopy it and read out the things you want, but I found it quite hard to read something, remembering what you want to pull out, pull it out and continue reading ... This is how I make a complete mess of things, people come in with one angle on things, and I come in with a completely different angle, it'll be the most obvious way as far as I'm concerned. I will explain something in a lecture and people will look and think, 'Hmm!', then 5 minutes later someone else will explain exactly what I meant, then they'll go, 'That's brilliant that's exactly what we are looking for', and I'll go, 'That's just what I've said'.

What sort of text do you find difficult to read?

Some education things that I'm meant to be reading, I'll start read-ing and think, 'yes this is really good', then I'll have to go back to the beginning. What I tend to do is read it, put it down and pick it up again, read the same paragraph and not realise that I'd read the same paragraph about four times.

So is it hard to keep a character in your mind, when they keep introducing a new person?

I'm all right, it depends on the style of the book, I quite like reading.

Are you a slow reader compared with your friends who are reading the same book?

I'm slow in comparison with some of them, but not particularly. I can read sentences, but not particularly take them in.

How about spelling?

Spelling is not that bad. Things like weather, hoping, hopping – I have a big problem with that. I'm not convinced when they've got two 'p's in them, or 'c's, or 'advise' and 'advice'. I'm not very good at distinguishing subtle differences between letters. I find, because I teach children, they'll ask me for something really simple like how do you spell 'brown' and I get it completely wrong, and I find the second I start panicking about it I can't spell anything. Sometimes I spell words phonetically.

Have you told any tutors about your difficulties and, if so, what was their response?

I told one and she said write it on to each essay and we will take it into account, which I thought was quite good. I've written on my essays 'please take into account my dyslexia', but the first essay I did was terribly bad. I did it on computer with the spellchecker and some of the words were the right spelling of a different word.

Do you think the word processor is powerful enough to pick up the mistakes?

Yes, but things like minute and minuet. The spellchecker displays a list of possible words, and I still don't know which one is correct. At college last year they said they weren't going to have any more dyslexic students becoming teachers, and I was thinking that I can help a child who has learning difficulties better than someone who hasn't.

The positive side of your dyslexia is having chosen teaching as a career you can be more empathic.

In some ways I think I'm like that anyway, because I know ways I've helped myself.

Do you get funding from the LEA [local education authority] and how do you use it?

I got £3500, which I bought a computer with. They are giving me a grant, they gave it to me last year, but not this year. They gave me a grant and said it was for extra study, useful things like that, and they said I can apply for extra money when I need help.

Ideally, what sort of support do you think should be available for dyslexic students?

I think that it is publicity that is important. When I told my teachers that I was attending the talk you gave on investigating dyslexia at university, their response was negative and they said 'Oh you're not dyslexic are you?' They shouldn't have this attitude, they're supposed to be teachers. But I think that student services should be better publicised. Personally, I would like to meet other dyslexic students at the university, to share ideas.

What strategies have you found effective in helping you deal with your work? Do you use any particular techniques or strategies?

I actually get things organised first. I bought myself a file and I write down everything I do for each subject, then I write down everything I do each week. That was just my attempt to get it so that my work wasn't in piles, a structure where everything was.

Do you use any technology such as a word processor, spellchecker or a dictaphone?

A spellchecker. I used to take it to school with me, you type it how you think it's spelt.

Do you think that knowing you are dyslexic affects your confidence in your ability to do academic work?

I don't know. Sometimes it's better to know you're dyslexic than not to know it. At least I know it's not me being stupid, me being disorganised. When I was younger I was very unconfident, as I got older it hasn't bothered me so much.

How do you think your particular personality influences the way you deal with dyslexia? Or, conversely, has having dyslexia had an influence on how your personality has developed?

I wouldn't like to stand up and say in a lecture, necessarily, this is what I think. It's quite often I think it's probably completely wrong.

Has dyslexia affected your self-esteem?

Not knowing what dyslexia was did. People just think you are stupid and it makes you feel stupid. And not to know you're dyslexic, outside academic work, it makes you feel less sure about yourself. I wasn't really confident until I was about 15 or 16. Then I got to college and thought that it doesn't matter anymore.

When you were 15 or 16, were you aware what dyslexia was?

I didn't really know until last year. When I was 15 or 16 I met people who were cleverer than me and who weren't cleverer than me and it didn't matter. It made me think it wasn't my fault anyway, it's something in my head, even though I wasn't totally sure what it meant.

Do you tell other students you are dyslexic?

I told some, not all of them. I've told one or two people that I'm dyslexic. I'd like to tell everyone honestly. If it stops people from saying 'you're thick' or 'you're stupid', then I'll tell them all – but some people are a bit pathetic in my opinion. I've heard people on buses saying 'She's either really stupid or she's dyslexic'. And you *can* be clever *and* dyslexic ...You can overcome it. People can knock you totally by ridiculing you ... It makes me quite angry. People come out with all sorts of dyslexic jokes. People tell them and you turn round and tell them 'I am dyslexic' and they go 'Oh! sorry!' I think people should know about it.

Do you ask other students or staff for specific help? Do you ever get friends to read back a piece of work or check it?

My flatmate goes through my work and checks it for me. She goes through, dots the 'i's and crosses the 't's. My other one's completely useless. I think she could be dyslexic as well.

What about approaching teachers?

I haven't approached them for specific help. I wouldn't tell examiners. I did ask once if I could use a computer, but he said they would first have to take the cut and paste off, take the spellcheck off, and I said 'Hang on! You're going to let me type – there's no use with the spellcheck off'. I then talked them through it and eventually they said I could have the cut and paste. That was the whole point of me using a computer for structure. He didn't know what it meant. I haven't sat the exam yet, but I will do.

Are there any situations that you find particularly difficult or embarrassing because of your dyslexia, like writing cheques?

The most embarrassing thing I had to do was stand in a queue and ask someone how to spell 'sixty' and everyone looked at me, so I asked if they took Switch. And I forget to put things on cheques. Timetables; I spent hours looking at this timetable, it was to get from Liverpool to Newcastle and it was working out the times like 15:47. I don't like reading out loud.

How do you deal with times when you are writing work and someone is looking at you: is that a particular problem?

I tend to make my writing more illegible and people start looking at me and they can't make out what I'm writing. It's funny looking back at your notes and realising you've written an absolute pile of rubbish.

Have you ever felt isolated at university, or when you were younger, because of your dyslexia?

Yes, I have. It's quite frustrating.

Would you find it helpful to meet other dyslexics in any way?

I'd find it really interesting to talk to other dyslexic students, and realise that others have a similar problem. A lot of people have over-come things. It took me 3 and a half months to learn to juggle [tasks]. I couldn't tell the time until I was 15. I knew what time meant, but I just couldn't tell it at all. You'll meet people who've got the same thing as you. I found it quite helpful last year when another dyslexic student was on the same course as me and we'd sit in lessons, we'd sit there talking about it, and everyone else would look and think, 'What are they doing?' We'd describe lessons, and we'd know where we were up to.

Have you met anyone in the past or now who has ridiculed your dyslexia? You mentioned that your sister sometimes made fun of your dyslexia?

Last year she went out with a bloke who was dyslexic and she suddenly noticed that he would walk out of her entire life, like he would go down to the shops and not come back for 2 weeks. Then suddenly she noticed these things with me that she had never noticed before living with him – things like losing his shoes and it was just completely dyslexic.

Do you think dyslexia will have a bearing on the job that you do when leaving university?

I think it might do, I intend to get my degree hopefully, then I want to go round the world; I don't want to stay in Britain. Then I want to teach. I hated school, so I want to go back and change completely. So the children I teach come back thinking she was great rather than useless.

So do you anticipate dyslexia will give you difficulties in teaching?

I think organisation, report writing, assessment and lesson planning. The thing is I'm great when I'm actually talking to the children, and the best lesson I ever did was when I went in with one idea for 5 minutes and the lesson lasted an hour and a half, so I made the rest up off the top of my head. The stuff that came out. I did letter writing, addressing envelopes, addressing letters, and all the work that came out of it, the teacher was really impressed and said you must have thought really hard about that. It was really good, I differentiated with the children whilst I was going along. If I had to write it down I would never have got the ideas. I'd be all right, but a teacher taking over, if I had time off, would be completely useless because nobody would be able to take over what I was doing. I never sat down and wrote it, but the way it worked out was really good, it was really structured, it fitted with everything I was doing, it wasn't planned at all.

In general, how do you feel at the moment about being dyslexic?

In some ways I'm not cleverer, but I'm as clever as a hell of a lot of people, but I just think in a completely different way, I think people should realise dyslexics think in a different way. I'm not like my sister, who just sort of writes and researches and she's really good at doing things that way. I'm totally different; I just do it and I can't research, but I'm just as good as her.

Comment

Effects of the label

'It made me think it wasn't my fault anyway, it's something in my head, even though I wasn't totally sure what it meant.' Caroline finds the idea that she is dyslexic helpful, because she feels that she does not have to blame herself for her lack of organisation. On the other hand, her encounters with the world when she has used the label to obtain support have not always been particularly helpful. 'At school I was called stupid and dyslexia was not recognised.' 'At college last year they said they weren't going to have any more dyslexic students becoming teachers.' 'People can knock you totally by ridiculing you ... It makes me quite angry. People come out with all sorts of dyslexic jokes.'

What is dyslexia?

In Caroline's interview, the question that continually surfaces seems to be 'What is dyslexia?' Caroline had some difficulties learning to read and spell initially and now has some reading and spelling problems – but to her these are not the major source of her difficulties. She dwells at far greater length on the problems of organisation – of her life and of her studies and written work. 'But the way that I do everything, the complete lack of organisation is to do with dyslexia.' She sees herself as having overcome any earlier difficulties with reading and spelling to be left with difficulties that are not classically termed 'dyslexic'. She talks of dyslexia as a problem that pervades her social life as much as or even more than her academic life, and a clear message comes through of her need to prove herself in her adult life – as someone who failed the 11-plus and went to a school where many pupils had difficulties with literacy.

Current research into the difficulties of dyslexic pupils suggests that many dyslexics have difficulties not only with literacy, but also with other tasks involving motor co-ordination. Recent research seems to provide increasing evidence that developmental reading and language disorders are neurologically based and may be due to the disruption of specific neurological processing mechanisms (Anderson, Brown and Tallal, 1993). The consequences of this disruption are not purely in relation to literacy but also to a wide range of tasks involving reaction times, information processing and motor control. Adults identified as dyslexic in childhood consistently show a wide range of functional differences when compared with non-dyslexics (Moore et al, 1995; Brachacki, Nicholson and Fawcett, 1995). Anecdotal reports from such adults often feature in discussions of the problems of self-organisation.

Self-motivation

It is clear from Caroline's account that she sees her achievements to be the consequence of her own determination to succeed. 'I taught myself to read because I had this system where I said, "I am not going to be stupid."' Her parents were sympathetic to her difficulties but evidently did not emphasise to her the fact that these were not due to her own lack of effort. She appears to have gone through her school and further education careers with a vague notion that she was dyslexic but with no clear idea of what this might signify. This lack of clarity may have been due to the milder nature of her reading and spelling problems and the consequent lack of emphasis on the other possible features of the problem. It seems clear, however, that Caroline was and remains determined to show the world that she is not stupid. 'You *can* be clever *and* dyslexic ... You can overcome it.'

Environmental factors

Caroline sees herself as succeeding despite her school environment. It seems that her schools either did not recognise her problem or offered support that she found inappropriate. Her failure in the 11-plus and her sister's evident, contrasting, success were clearly important factors in her life. A continuing emphasis on sibling rivalry and the comparison between her own and her sister's ability suggest that this was an important factor in shaping her self-image and in spurring on her own efforts. Shared genetic make-up and shared immediate family environment lend themselves to a comparison of differences. Any differences between siblings are naturally emphasised, and uncomfortable comparisons may work to the detriment of the developing self-image and self-esteem of a less able or disabled sibling (Harter, 1990). Caroline's score on the Self-Esteem Inventory was extremely low, suggesting that, despite her success relative to other dyslexics, she has internalised a model of herself as lacking in worth.

Chapter 8
Sean

'I truly thought I was thick and just couldn't do it. I did give up... and I spent the first and second year of secondary school in town. I didn't go in. I just stopped going in.'

Sean is a 22-year-old student doing a degree in optoelectronics. His score on the Adult Dyslexia Checklist suggests a severe impairment. Although his spelling is poor, it is not very poor. His scores on the psychometric tests suggest that his self-esteem is low, his state anxiety intermediate, but his trait anxiety high.

The Interview

Do you think the experiences you had before coming to university are affecting the way you are coping now? Talk about your experiences at school.

Well, I always hated school. At school I always thought I was dyslexic. Parents thought I was. School totally rejected the idea. They thought I was just this idiotic moron. It started off when I was taken out of all my GCSEs, I got forced back in them.

When were you identified as being dyslexic?

It was 1993. I was 21.

When you were at school did any of your teachers recognise that you had dyslexia, or did they recognise that you were having problems and how did they deal with it?

They recognised a problem. I was in set one for maths and I was in remedial class for English.

What age were you then?

Fourteen, but they just never did anything about it. They tried to give me help with English but never anything like saying I was dyslexic or I've got specific problem. I just couldn't do it.

Did you have any problems at primary school?

Supposedly, I could read before I went to school. I didn't learn to write until I was about 11. I never really started reading books until I came to university. I couldn't read a book before then.

What kinds of difficulty did you experience at secondary school?

It was because I wasn't sure of being dyslexic and I was thought of as being thick. I wasn't given much help. I was put in with the rest of the morons that didn't want to work. So here's me trying to work and there's people jumping out of the classroom window. It was a nightmare really.

So, none of the teachers recognised that you had any difficulties whatsoever?

No. Just the fact that I had difficulty and I couldn't do English.

Did your parents recognise that you had difficulties at all?

They always thought there was something wrong. They thought I was dyslexic because that's the most obvious conclusion.

At what age were you formally assessed?

I was 21.

No one at your school mentioned you were dyslexic?

My mother mentioned it. I did have a strange sort of test and I was taken by one of the teachers sticking bits of coloured sheet on top of writing, and you sort of thought 'That doesn't make any difference'. This consisted of 5 minutes.

Before you were assessed, what did you think of yourself and why did you think you were having these difficulties?

I truly thought I was thick and just couldn't do it. I did give up. It wasn't for the fact that I was bad in English. It was for the fact that I was dyslexic. [I said] 'Sod this at school', and I spent [the] first and second year of secondary school in town. I didn't go in. I just stopped going in. I wasn't kicked out. Then I would boot my ideas back in but still I didn't think. I was forced to go in. Once I got the assessment, it was like one of the greatest days ever. It was just like, 'Yes, I'm not thick'.

Did knowing that you were dyslexic change the way you saw yourself and did this have any effect on your academic work?

It seemed to have, since I failed the second year. Found out I had this [dyslexia] when I got a work placement. Whenever something came up that I couldn't do, I just threw it on the carpet and said 'I can't do it'. Doing physics there is a lot of research and somebody has to go and get these journals and pick them up from the libraries and after 20 minutes it used to give me a headache. I used to knock off after 20 minutes and I use to tell the boss that I just couldn't do it, and he accepted it. He gave me manuals about the lasers and how they worked. I gave them back saying 'There is no way I can work through them. Could you just show us?' I said I'd come back as well. I seemed to be doing a hell of a lot better.

So, your confidence has improved since your assessment?

Yes.

Has this affected relationships with other people at all, before and after the assessment?

On a personal level, no. I've never had problems at all. I've never had problems talking.

Did you receive any additional help or support for your dyslexia? You mentioned you had remedial help at school and that didn't help.

Six attempts to get a GCSE. I moved up one grade to a 'C' every step of the way.

Was that at school or college?

At school. Every chance I got in the sixth form. Every time there was a resit of an exam I was taking it and failing it.

Are you receiving any additional help at the moment?

No. I am going to get dyslexic lessons once the local education authority get organised and start paying fees for the place, and getting extra time in exams.

While you were in post-16 education, how did you cope with your work and what kind of strategies did you use to help you overcome [your problems]?

If it came to reading something out, I'd read it out as if somebody else read it. From them reading it to explaining it to me. Trying whenever I can not [to] write sentences but in statements and points.

In general, do you feel that your family have been supportive or unsupportive with dealing with dyslexia?

They were supportive. They tried to help me with it.

Brothers and sisters?

One sister.

Dyslexic?

Down's syndrome.

Any previous generations?

I'm definitely sure my dad's dyslexic. Badly dyslexic, but he's never been tested. It just sticks out like a sore thumb.

What are the indicating signs?

You name it, he's got it. A perfect example is he writes everything back to front and the wrong way round. His reading's atrocious, his writing's terrible, he's clumsy.

Your grandparents at all?

Nothing past that.

Why did you choose to study at this University?

Nobody else would take me. I failed my ' A ' levels, took them again and failed them.

When you were applying to university was dyslexia an issue?

No, I was still not aware of dyslexia.

Was it a consideration with support services?

I couldn't do English and that was the end of it.

Turning to the present, do you think the sorts of problem you face at university are much the same as other students'? What is specific about your problems as opposed to a non-dyslexic student?

Talking in classes, that's no problem. I find that I actually get better marks because I cannot read off a bit of paper. If I read off a piece of paper in a presentation then you are marked down straight away, so I learn before I go in and don't bother with prompt cards or anything. I just make it up as I go along.

So, thinking on your feet is not a problem?

No, it's no problem, but it's just reading and writing, the speed of it.

So, would you say it would take you twice as long to comprehend than others?

Some passages I can't comprehend at all. When it comes to factual maths books and physics books it just doesn't go in, full stop. I can look at it for hours and it still wouldn't go in. I just can't do it. Lack of concentration. I can't do that at all. I just try to skim it to get the briefest outline of whatever it is trying to say to me, putting things in my own words because a lot of our stuff is the theory behind it. You'll be writing an essay on the theory that's all [been] done before. When everyone's got a book about it you're not putting much of yourself in, but you can't copy out of a book so you've got to write it in your own words. So I'd read a passage and there's no way I can write it in my own words. I always copy it straight out word for word and if I'm picked up for it I am going to say, 'He writes it better than I can'. It wouldn't make sense if I tried to write it, so there's no point.

Has that always been a problem?

Yes, it has.

In what ways do you think having dyslexia is affecting your academic work. For example, reading?

Reading out loud, or even reading in my head. Reading out loud was impossible. I'll get two lines before it's gone and I've lost where I am.

Do the words appear to move on the page?

Yes, and jump between the lines. I'll come to an end of a line and I'll be two lines down and between those I'll start moving up and down the lines.

So the problem is you'll jump a word. Maybe that's because you're having problems comprehending text, because you might miss a word and you tend to jump ahead. How about your assignments at the moment? Would you say you have to work twice as hard writing an essay?

A lot more than twice as hard for writing an essay.

Do you have any problems handing work in on time, or do you ask for many extensions?

Apart from laziness, no. We are given enough time to do it.

Have you told your tutors about your dyslexia?

Yes.

And what was their response?

'What a good con to get a computer, wangled in next year's grant', because I used dyslexia as a way to getting part of next year's grant[1]. Just a big con really. Everyone takes it as a bit of a joke. I had to push like mad to get the extra half hour. They weren't going to give it to me.

Did you approach them as soon as you had your assessment done?

I think I went and told them I was dyslexic but by the time I was assessed I was going on placement, so I wasn't really in contact with them. As soon as I got back, then I did. Some of them are more helpful than others but when I tried to get set notes off one of them, he said his writing was too long. I think he talked to the head of the year because he's in the dyslexics' association and said, 'I'll push as well if you really want these notes'. He was going to give me them. Then they changed their mind. They said if you found one lecturer was going too fast then you could photocopy that set [of] notes afterwards. They wouldn't give me the set notes so I could sit in the lecture and could understand what he was saying.

Is that from when he is using acetate sheets on the board and taking information down from the acetate sheets?

It would help if he photocopied that material and you could sit with that material in front of you and you could write notes while he is talking. That's the thing. He has got them on the board and he is talking all of the time.

What other support from tutors would you appreciate?

I'm not sure. I can't believe [that] for one person in the class that you can alter the structure, so I don't really know. It's just help and guidance when you really need it and awareness of a problem.

Your'e getting funding from the Local Education Authority. Could you talk a bit about how you are using it?

I've got my computer and a printer with spellchecker, and type things out because I type faster than I write. I'm going to get a software package so I can scan the text.

Can you tell me briefly how that would be [of]help to your work?

With the use of the scanner I could actually read and understand what the books were actually saying instead of looking at a set of text and not comprehending it all.

So I presume you could scan the material from notes and take that into a package that could read it out?

That's what it's for. I can also read out my own text, writing out my own package for an essay. It [my essay] doesn't make sense because the commas and full stops and punctuation are in the wrong place. I'll read it back and it'll sound like gobbledy gook, so I'm going to sit and try to put the commas and full stops into the right place.

How is the spellchecker for the kind of mistakes that you make? Is it powerful enough to pick them up?

Yes, it picks up a lot of them, but it hasn't got any scientific words. I'm just going to have to sit and check them. My dad's got this great package, but I am unable to find it. It actually beeps when you get the word wrong. You can actually be halfway through a word and if that does not join in a word it will actually beep and it won't stop beeping until you get the word right.

How about the grammar check?

I can't get the hang of that. There's too many things inpassive voices and I don't understand adjectives anyway. So I think I've got my head round nouns and things, so far.

What aspects of your work do you feel you excel in?

Presentations is one.[In] presentations [I] don't usually get under 90%. I'm doing all right though in reports that aren't essay-based and [in] the other two bits in language. Anything I can take away and spend time on. Exams are where I fail really and, because of the set time, forgetting things I know. I need prompts. I'll sit down with the derivation, I know half the derivation, but I'll only know it from half-way down. I can never remember the first line.

What strategies have you found effective in helping you deal with your work?

Computer.

Do you use memory techniques or certain ways of how to spell a word?

I don't know. I probably do, but I don't set out to do things. Talking about it, I suppose. If I banter work backwards and forwards with someone I can learn a hell of a lot. Getting rid of books and things completely and talking about something.

Do you think that knowing that you are dyslexic affects your confidence in your ability to do academic work?

Yes, I've got a hell of a lot more confidence. If I'm going to sit down and write something then I am a lot more confident. Before, I would deliberately keep away from it. When it comes to reading out loud; I would never ever do anything like that, but now I will and I will make a complete mess of it. A few weeks ago I was sitting with a friend's little sister, a 9 year old, and we were reading poems out of a kiddie's book and her reading age is a lot higher than mine, and she was doing a hell of a lot better than I was doing. Once upon a time I would never do that, but nowadays I have no problem with that.

How do you think your particular personality influences the way you deal with dyslexia? Or, conversely, has having dyslexia had an influence on how your personality has developed?

Not really, it hasn't changed my personality.

Going back to school, you didn't know you were dyslexic, were there any behavioural problems that you had experienced, were you in a remedial group?

I suppose I was always a good boy. I never went around making trouble. I knocked around with bad lads but I would never make trouble.

Your absenteeism from school, was that quite frequent?

I didn't turn up.

Was it the third or the fourth year?

Near the start of the year they said, 'You've got to read this book'. We started to read in class. Luckily, I wasn't the first one and I never turned back up for most of the year. I just never turned up at the class at all. I think I turned up right at the end. There was a letter, my mother was in, and all sorts of stuff. They did help me a little bit because, at the end [when] we had to do an oral, I did that personally, not in front of the class. I had a real confidence thing. I was a really quiet kid.

Does having dyslexia affect your general self-esteem and, if so, in what way?
I don't think so. I feel better knowing I'm dyslexic.

A positive label?
Oh yes, definitely positive.

You perceive dyslexia as being a positive influence?
I don't care. I tell everyone with a big neon flashing light. It's a good thing to actually be labelled it than not be labelled it, because you've still got the same problems whether labelled or not. It's perceived in a better way knowing you're dyslexic than not knowing you're dyslexic. If you just can't read they thought I was thick. [It's] actually a reason for not being able to read.

Do you tell other students that you are dyslexic? Is that a particular problem?
No, it's not a problem at all.

Has anyone reacted badly to that?
No, not at all.

How would you deal with the situation if you told someone you were dyslexic and they laughed and made bad comments? How would you deal with that?
It wouldn't touch me at all.

Self-esteem and confidence?
No, I was knocked to shit while I was at the school. I can ride anything now, probably think of some decent comment back.

Do you ever ask other students or staff for specific help like proof reading some work?
Yes, when it comes to essays and letters. Things like that. Always proof read letters before they're sent away. I never ever write a letter and send it. It would be a ridiculous thing to do.

How about approaching staff for specific help? Do you feel comfortable about going up to a member of the staff and saying, 'Look I'm dyslexic'?

I feel comfortable. I spend my life with the head of year, we've got this tendency, we hate each other. He really hates me, so now I've got this nice job as a class rep, and now I'm making his life hell. So my dyslexic thing, any problems with the class he's dealing with, usually I'm quite [obstreperous] anyway, so it all rolls into one thing. So [I] go and see them. There's things I'm usually having problems with myself anyway.

Are there any situations that you find particularly difficult or embarrassing because of your dyslexia? This relates to everyday life not just academic work.

Reading things wrong, getting things back to front. Important things like train platform numbers, train times. I do the organising and get someone organised [for] the train and it'll turn up an hour later. That kind of thing. That's happened many times before.

What about names and faces, is that a particular problem?

I remember people's faces but never remember the names. I'm kind of left out by deliberately not learning anyone's name. I'm class rep, and I don't know anyone's name. Everyone thinks I know their name. I only know about five or six people on the course. Everyone else is just a face.

What about writing cheques in a shop? Is that a problem?

I don't like that kind of thing. I fill out a form in a shop and when somebody's actually looking at what you are writing I feel like poking them in the eye.

So you felt quite anxious and self-aware? Is there anything else that's a hindrance, meeting deadlines?

Oh! yes, you're lucky I'm here. If it hadn't been for turning round and asking a student when my appointment for this thing was and him saying its one o'clock on Tuesday. He had to remind me it's Tuesday today and it's one o'clock. I'd totally forgotten.

Have you ever felt isolated at university, or when you were younger, because of your dyslexia?

Until I went for the assessment, because that's how I found out. A friend went for a test and we got talking to him about it. I thought 'This sounds like it could be me'.

Directly after your assessment, you were reading your report and you thought,

Right, I'm 'this person, I am dyslexic'. Would it help if you knew any other dyslexics in the university?

Yes, just to go over how they overcome it. Any problems they are having. Just a pool of knowledge kind of thing. Maybe things I haven't thought of that could be a help.

When you were at school you didn't know it was dyslexia. Did you feel any isolation there?

I felt isolated from other people because I never fitted into any group. I was in group one for maths, all the swots in the maths class, and a remedial class for English, so neither side wanted me that badly, so I didn't belong to one group or the other.

Did you know any dyslexic students at all?

He's gone now.

If you hadn't met up with that dyslexic student, would you have known about the support services in the university?

No, I've been here since the foundation year. So I've been here 3 years almost and heard nothing about it at all.

Anything about support services or extra time in examinations?

No, nothing at all.

Do you anticipate that having dyslexia will give you any difficulties once you've left university?

Yes, it's something I've got for the rest of my life and it's not going to go or get better. Got to learn to cope with it.

So how do you feel about being dyslexic?

I answered that before, saying that I'd rather not be dyslexic, but I am dyslexic and it's better knowing.

Knowing you're dyslexic has improved your confidence and your ability to do academic work?

Definitely, yes.

So sometimes you might get frustrated because you have to work two or three times as hard as other people, but that frustration is not enough to make you say, 'Look, I'm going to pack it in'?

No, I've always had to fight for everything so far, so I'm not going to give up fighting now.

Comment

Sean's school experiences are somewhat unusual, given his age. His education spans a period from the mid 1970s to the present, a time when dyslexia has been increasingly recognised as a medico-educational condition. His experiences are more those of an older person: being placed in a remedial class, regarded as being stupid, lazy or both, and not being diagnosed until 21, when on the second year of a university course. Is he someone the system failed?

He reports having always had great difficulties with reading, writing, comprehension, and words moving, losing his place, lack of concentration, problems with punctuation and sentence construction and poor memory for information just read: all classic, specific symptoms of dyslexia. Sean also reports more general symptomatology, related to everyday life. He has problems with forms, confuses train times and platforms, cannot remember names and misses appointments. It seems clear that there is also a familial problem: his sister has Down's syndrome and his father is probably also dyslexic. Why was he missed?

One possible reason is that his behaviour may have provided the relevant people with other explanations. He frequently truanted and, even though he himself was not one, seems to have mixed with 'bad lads'. To what extent these characteristics were a function of the frustrations of dyslexia or of a naturally ebullient and forceful personality is difficult to gauge. Probably both, but they may have been enough to mask the true problem. On the other hand, it seems surprising that no one was struck by his fierce determination to succeed. He sat his public exams several times, probably in the face of sustained ridicule and humiliation, and was then determined to come to university, where he must have known things would not get much better.

In conclusion, Sean seems to be someone who slipped through the net. We hope that cases like his are now to become a rarity.

Notes

1 Sean failed and had to resit his second year. He would not normally have got a local authority grant for this extra year.

Chapter 9
Patrick

'At the minute I don't think I do well in anything, I'm doing really badly in the course and I'm not sleeping well and I'm missing lectures.'

Patrick is a 24-year-old student taking a degree in mechanical engineering. His score fell into the low category on the Culture Free Self-Esteem Inventory, and he received scores that put him into the high category for both state and trait anxiety. His interview closely reflected these scores, with him stressing his lack of confidence on several occasions, and in the latter part of the interview talking about his current state of anxiety over his studies. Unlike most of the students in the study, Patrick did not mention any early difficulties at primary school but, as he points out, he is not sure if this was necessarily the case or whether he simply does not remember.

The Interview

Well, I never really noticed anything different at primary school. The first few years (primary 1 to primary 5) there was never any real difference. I didn't notice any difference, maybe because it was so long ago that I can't remember that much about it. But the first memory I have of being different would be when I was in primary 6.

How old were you then?

I was about 10 or 11. And it was time for the 11-plus and the class was divided into three groups; there was the group that was expected to do really well, and there was another intermediate group who were expected to get a pass at least and a few might fail, and then there was a third group, which was the group I was in, and that was just basically the slow people's group. I found that the teacher did not have much time for us, I think there were over 30 kids in the class and he [the teacher] mainly dedicated his time to the people who were going to do the 11-plus, because these were the people whose figures were going to come up; saying this, many people passed. He was exerting all the time on these people. I remember we used to do mock 11-plus exams. I used to dread it, especially when we got the marks; the most I ever got was about 20 % or something stupid, and I regularly got those low marks. I thought I was stupid, the teacher would say, 'here's some maths problems, do these questions', although it was just simple addition I found myself wandering off, I was supposed to be working but I wasn't. The thing that I really remember was English, I used to find the readers that we used to read were very boring. I used to like to listen to the other group reading because the teacher would call each group round the table, and they would each read what they had prepared the night before and I was more interested in what they were doing. I could tell you everything about anyone else's reader, but I couldn't tell you anything about the book that I was reading. It just didn't happen. I remember one book we had to read, *Mr Fox*, we had a paragraph to prepare for the next day and I remember my parents grinding it into me. I was reading this paragraph and it was going right over my head, I wasn't picking anything up, and my parents were going over the story. In it there was a rhyme about 'Bogus, Bunce and Bean', in fact I still remember it:

> Bogus, Bunce and Bean,
> one short, one fat, one lean,
> was horrible crooks with different looks
> were no less equally mean,

and I remember that because my parents stood over me [until I learnt it]. They said, 'Pat, look, this is a rhyme, it's a poem'. I didn't know it was a poem. I had read it four times, it was just words, it didn't mean anything. I'm 24 now, it's nearly 14 years ago, and I can still remember that as if it were yesterday. I went into school the next day and it was the best I'd ever prepared anything, but they didn't notice. I thought 'shit'. I'd spent all my time doing this, my parents helped me so much and they couldn't give a damn. I suddenly thought, 'what is the point?'

What kind of difficulties did you experience in secondary school?

After I went to primary school we moved over the border to the Republic of Ireland and I had to do another year of national school, and they do 8 years in a primary school before going to secondary. We moved over the border and I went to another school, an old-fashioned kind of school although the class wasn't too big [about 25 people in the class] and I was the new boy, I was the centre of attention. The headmaster taught me in sixth class, we were doing reading and he asked me to read out; obviously I had a lot of difficulty reading it, when everyone else was reading it straight off very well. It was like climbing hurdles and he said, 'I want you to come to me after lunch time', and he would take me for reading practice. He would give me a page and I would go home and prepare it, and come back next day and read it. That was the first time anyone had ever really said 'look here, you not doing so well, let me help you'. The first teacher who actually wanted to help me. I didn't like him, I hated him, but he was the only teacher that did show an interest.

Did that motivate you at all?

Not really, because it took up most of my lunch time, but I knew it was doing me good so I did it.

Did any of the other teachers identify a problem in primary school?

When I left primary school the headmaster said, 'Look, if you want to come and talk to me I'll tell you what I think of you and what I think you're going to do'. But I wouldn't go because I knew subconsciously what he was going to say, but my dad went to see him at the end. He came back and said, 'Pat, your headmaster said that you can't draw, you can't write English, you can't do maths. Pat', he said, 'the best thing I can do for you is to buy you a bucket, a ladder and sponge then you can clean windows for the rest of your life'. That to me was like this headmaster had told me that I was stupid, that I was beyond redemption. There are smart people and stupid people and, like, I was a stupid person.

Was dyslexia ever mentioned?

No, it was never mentioned then, but when I went on to national school in the Republic dyslexia was mentioned, but only as a translation in Irish, that was the first time I'd heard it. The Irish language is an old language, there aren't words for 'helicopter' for instance, they don't exist in the Irish language. Dyslexia translated for me meant reading words sideways. For example, someone writes 'saw' and you read 'was'. I wasn't dyslexic because when I wrote 'was' I read 'was'. The first mention of dyslexia was when I went into secondary school which was in the Republic of Ireland. I went through the first 3 years and did the intercert. Everyone was telling me to do my best, 'we're not expecting the best of you'. At the time I was really keen on wind-surfing and my dad said, 'Pat, if you pass your intercert I'll buy you a sailboard, all the gear. Show me the results that you pass and I'll buy it for you.' So I went to school and worked a bit and read hard, and did the intercert.

What exactly is the intercert?

It's something like 'O' levels; you do eight subjects and I got one 'B', two 'C's and five 'D's and all of these are considered passes ... I got the 'B' in Science, I got a 'C' in Mechanical Drawing, I did Metal Work and I got a 'C' in that, and I got 'D's in Commerce, English and Maths, History and Geography.

Were you formally assessed as dyslexic at secondary school?

It was just after that. What happened was dyslexia became trendy, it became like a buzzword, it wasn't reading words wrongly or side-ways it was an actual learning disability; there was a problem here and you weren't stupid and you didn't see things that were not there. This teacher, a careers guidance officer, said 'Pat, I want you to see an educational psychologist'.

How old were you then?

Between 15 and 16.

Before the educational psychologist stated that you have dyslexia, what did you think of yourself and why did you think you were having these difficulties?

When I was really young I was always quiet and withdrawn and I was always in a world of my own, and the teachers commented to my parents that I was a loner, that I seemed withdrawn from everything. I basically put it down to me being stupid, because that's what the teachers said to me in the primary school. Teachers had indicated that they were not willing to spend time with me because I was not doing so well. I've seen other people doing better than me and I thought.'Oh well, they're doing well and I'm doing badly. So they must be smart and I must be stupid', and I was convinced that I was an idiot.

How about your friends?

Actually, my friends were in the other two groups that were above me. I had friends in the intermediate group who were fairly normal.

Then the other group, the academic group, I found that I could get on with people regardless of the group they were in. But I just didn't have the scope to do the work that they were doing but I could communicate with them verbally and they were good friends.

Did knowing that you were dyslexic change the way you saw yourself?

I remember after I had seen the educational psychologist I got the results back, it was like a massive weight had lifted off my shoulders and suddenly I wasn't stupid anymore. It was like someone had tapped me on the shoulder and said 'look, you're not stupid anymore, you're smart'. What made me feel really good was that the psychologist had said to me that part of the test was a test of general knowledge, and that you have answered some questions that I don't remember anyone else answering correctly before. And I felt, 'I'm not stupid, I know these answers'. One of the questions was, 'what is one of the minerals that aluminium is refined from?' and I knew it was bauxite. I didn't even have to think about it and he looked kind of surprised. I felt great.

After the assessment was made, did you receive any additional help or support?

Well, the teachers knew I was dyslexic, and I did get special compensation. For example, with written work like business organisation or English we had to write essay-type answers. I was given an envelope with instructions that I should not be penalised for poor spelling and poor grammar, they would look for the ideas in the text rather than penalise me for silly mistakes. They would look for the intelligent structure in it. It was fairly close to the exam when I got the results back.

Was it too late for time concessions in examinations?

There was nothing really they could have done, it was just up to me to learn the material.

What was your parents' attitude to you being diagnosed as dyslexic?

They were kind of relieved, because they were convinced that they had an idiot son. But they found out that he was not an idiot, and he was intelligent. It was just that I [he] thought differently to everyone else. They never really said anything else, I think they were guilty, because they had thought that I was unintelligent, and I wasn't. It was the teachers who were the idiots, they made the mistakes because they didn't see it.

How did you cope with the academic work after school? What kind of strategies did you use?

After school I went on to do a BTec in Engineering, there was no real written work involved, maybe just a paragraph. They let the spelling mistakes slip here. But I didn't actually pass my diploma, I failed it; I'd dropped two units at the end, although I was offered a place at Newcastle to do a foundation year, and I did that.

In general, do you think your family have been supportive or unsupportive in dealing with your dyslexia?

I am not really sure if it was support; it was like I was their son and I was going to do whatever I had to do myself whatever happened. I think that they were relieved to find out that I wasn't stupid. But they never really spoke to me about it or said anything about it. I didn't really need their support because I knew that I was dyslexic. I remember the biggest disappointment that I ever got was when the teacher said 'Oh, you're dyslexic, don't worry about that because lots of people have that', and I thought I was unique.

Have you got any brothers or sisters, and are they dyslexic too?

Yes, one brother.

Is he dyslexic?

No, he is very intelligent, he is younger than me. He is the rebel of the family, but doesn't apply himself. He's always got a scam working.

Why did you choose to study at this university?

I applied to quite a few places. I flicked through the book [on degree courses] and it stopped at Newcastle for Applied Physics and I thought, 'I'll do that'. But I thought applied physics was something different, the physics that they talked about was solid-state physics and I thought it was more mechanics. But I came here to do the foundation, the electronic and electrical engineering course. I passed that straight away, sailed through that, and went on to mechanical engineering.

Was your dyslexia ever a consideration when applying to university?

In the foundation it was. I said to my tutor 'I'm dyslexic', and she pulled out my file and noted that I was dyslexic, and that was that.

She said to do my best, 'complete all the assignments, and if I find some of the assignments are borderline then I will take that into consideration. But if you pass straight through anyway we don't need to bring it up. If you pass, you pass; if you don't, we'll review the situation.'

Do you think that the problems that you face at university are much the same as other students'?

I do get really disheartened, I put a lot of work into things like lab reports, assignments and things that do have a lot of writing to do. I get them back and they say 'good attempt, spoilt by bad spelling and poor grammar'. There are red marks on all of the spelling mistakes and it always says 'good effort, shame about the spelling'. Even if I do things on a word processor, there are some words that I have a massive mental block on, like the word 'companies', I would run it through the spellchecker and it would give me a couple of suggestions, and I didn't know which one to choose, so I thought right 'I'll go for that one'.

Are you able to keep up with other students taking notes?

I find it difficult to keep up with the lecturers writing something on the board, I find that I'm always racing to keep up. When everyone else is at the stage to move on I'm still stuck behind, trying to scribble it down.

How about reading your notes afterwards?

Usually I can read it, if I work at it a bit. Sometimes there maybe a few things that don't look right, but not very often.

How about the time it takes you to complete work?

I have a lot of difficult in structuring words together that explain something, just fitting words together; usually I just write facts, single line, short facts, one after another. Then to turn something like that into a paragraph, and then into an explanation or a report, that's what I find difficult. It's making the connection between each point and introducing things at the right time. I write short, concise sentences and try and say [what I mean] in one sentence.

Have you told any of your tutors about your dyslexia and, if so, what was their reaction?

I told a lecturer that I was dyslexic and that I was having some problems with the course, and I said, 'I cannot really expect you to do anything about it because I have no documented evidence to say that I am and anyone can come up to you and say "Oh, I'm dyslexic". There is no way I can prove [it], I don't know how to get tested, but I have been tested but I can't get my hands on that assessment.'

Did your tutor suggest how you could get an assessment?

He did not know, there was nothing basically that he could do about it. I didn't expect that there was anything that he could do, but I just thought that I'd better tell somebody. I mean I couldn't prove that I was dyslexic, he couldn't disprove [it] and I didn't know how to get tested.

Did he tell you about support services at all?
No.

Are you currently receiving any support for your dyslexia?

The literacy centre in the library [WAND centre], I spoke to Ann [a support worker], she said that it would cost £250 to get tested and that if I wrote to the education authority that they would give me a grant to be tested, but a lot of education authorities don't because if they do, they have to give you money so that you can get a PC to do word processing. I'm not receiving any funding.

Ideally, what kind of support should be made available to dyslexic students?

I'm not really sure actually; me personally, I find it difficult to concentrate on work and maybe that's just me at the minute. Maybe to let people know it's not stupidity, but a different way of thinking, that's what I was told.

How about literacy support, where you could go to have your essays checked?

Something like that would be good, they could proofread your work, because even when I do word processing I still get them back with bad spelling mistakes and things that I have missed. Yes, which 'where' do I use, I mean I'd even spell it wrongly as well.

Do you spell words how they sound?

Yes, actually my frame of mind as well depends on it, how I feel at the time. I could be writing an essay and I would have the same word spelt three different ways and I wouldn't know which one was right, and I would think 'hang on, one of these is right' and I simply couldn't tell.

What aspects of your work do you think you do well in?

At the minute I don't think I do well in anything, I'm doing really badly in the course and I'm not sleeping well and I'm missing lectures. The more I miss lectures the more I worry about it. I've always had insomnia, but it seems to have got worse maybe because I've got more pressure now. But I lie awake at night and everything is flowing through my mind, things that I have done, things that I should have done, what I should be doing, the work that I have missed, and what little work I have done. I just can't sleep because I'm so worried that I have to do this work and I can't just switch off, go to sleep, tomorrow I'll wake up and start over again. So what happens is that I end up still awake at 6.00 a.m., and then I fall asleep. I've tried herbal sleeping remedies, my diet, stopped drinking coffee. But when I've stopped drinking coffee I had even less energy during the day.

Have you excelled in any areas of your course?

No, I do like energy studies but I wouldn't say that I excel in it in anyway.

What kind of strategies have you found effective in helping you deal with your work?

Copying from books is good. What I do is get a pencil and a few different books and underline sentences and I just basically copied from the books and sort of formed my own interpretation from these four or five different books (but don't tell my lecturers that).

Do you use any form of technology, and how useful do you find this?

I use the word processor in the library; it's quite useful because sometimes it spots stupid things like writing a word twice instead of once.

Is this repetition of words common?

Yes it is. Things like 'a', sometimes the spellcheck picks it up. Sometime it gives you four or five suggestions; the words are right in front of me and I just can't choose the right ones.

Do you think that knowing you are dyslexic affects you confidence in the ability to do work?

It affects my confidence in the fact that I know that I have to put more effort in than everyone else to get the same result, this is kind of offputting sometimes where I have to work harder than everyone else, just to get the same place they are. Confidence, I haven't got any confidence.

How do you think your particular personality influences the way you deal with your dyslexia?

I'm not really sure. I don't care who knows that I'm dyslexic, I'm not sensitive about it. I'm dyslexic, that's it; you could tell the world, I just don't care. Maybe that [attitude] in a way has affected my personality but if it has, it has affected it from when I was really young and just gone straight through, so I don't really notice any change.

Does having dyslexia affect your general self-esteem?

Yes. Basically, the fact that I've got to work harder. I can't read things aloud because I know that I'm going to make stupid mistakes, that I am going to sound really stupid trying to read this because I know that I can't do it. Writing letters, I hate writing letters. I only write letters to my close friends.

Do they know that you're dyslexic?

Yes.

Do you tell other students that you're dyslexic?

Yes, I do tell other students that I'm dyslexic, I don't know why, maybe because I'm an attention seeker.

What kind of response do you get when you tell others?

They say 'you what, really?', usually disbelief or surprise. It's like some rare, exotic disease.

Do you think that they understand what dyslexia is?

I think nowadays a lot of people understand dyslexia is more of a learning difficulty rather than just not seeing words that are there, and reading things wrong.

Do you ever ask other students or staff to proofread your work?

No, never.

For what reason?

I'm not embarrassed to admit I'm dyslexic, but I know it is going to be riddled with mistakes, maybe I don't handle criticism very well. The spelling mistakes that I make are really very stupid and I don't want anyone else to see them.

Do you re-read a piece of work that you have just written?

Each time I read it I have to stop myself from changing it because I know that I'll just change it and change it, like spellings and stuff, so usually I just write it and read it through and get it the best I can to the lecturer.

Are there any situations that you find particularly difficult or embarrassing because of your dyslexia?

Yes, writing cheques. I couldn't spell 'Arthur'. I had to write a check at Presto's, made payable to 'Arthur's Hill'. So I just smudged it, I wrote little squiggles to make it look like 'Arthur'. Spelling things like 'forty', other things like spelling 'forward' I have big problems with that. I have problems with 'always' until I saw the movie and after that I been able to spell it. Telling the time sometimes [can be difficult], the 12-hour clock, sometimes that hand will be lying in between two numbers and I'm not sure which numbers they are, like is it quarter to five or quarter to six, sort of in between [I don't know].

Have you ever felt isolated at university because of your dyslexia?

I've always tended to be alone. I've got quite a good friends, close friends, but most of them are elsewhere in Ireland or Liverpool. There are other friends who are kind of close. I feel lonely quite a lot, I don't know if that is me isolating myself because of my personality or because of the dyslexia. But I do find myself isolated and lonely, even with people I can talk to I feel isolated from them. People can talk to me and people tend to tell me things like their deepest darkest secrets that no one else is suppose to hear, really personal things; people tell of problems that they are having or things that they are suffering from, and I just know that, and they say 'how do you know that?', and I say 'I guessed it, you've just confirmed it for me', but when it comes the other way I can't talk to people, I can't tell them what's going on here. I can't really relate to other people.

Does that feeling perhaps stem from your experiences at school?

At school I was always a loner, I had few friends there. I went to the cubs and I had to leave the cubs because everyone was teasing me calling things like 'dreamboat', 'stupid' and 'sleepyhead', because I was always in my own world.

Do you ever meet with any other students who have dyslexia?

One or two people I've met think that they might be dyslexic but they're not sure. But they don't appear to me as dyslexic.

Would it be helpful to meet other dyslexic students?

Yes, speaking to someone else who is going through the same stuff that I'm going through, who feels really frustrated and fed up and what's the point?

Would that help your confidence?

Yes, to have someone to talk to, who is trying just as hard as me, if not harder.

Have you ever met anyone in the past or now who has ridiculed your dyslexia, and, if so, how did you cope with that?

No one has ever really ridiculed me for my dyslexia, but I have been ridiculed for not being able to read things. I'll look at something and I'll read it and it won't be what's written down and then people would laugh and say 'Are you blind?' or something, and then I'll say 'Oh shit, I didn't see that properly'. But no one has ever really ridiculed me for being dyslexic. I don't know how I would react if someone did, I might become oversensitive and take it to heart or I might just lash out and do some damage. I don't know.

Do you think that your dyslexia will have any kind of bearing on the kind of job you do when you leave university?

Well, I hope to go into engineering and secretaries are an excellent invention, so I'll utilise that as much as possible. They can write and type.

Do you anticipate that dyslexia will give you any difficulties when you leave university?

I think that when I do leave university the difficulty will not be as it has been at university. Life will become easier after I get out of here. Although I don't think that I'm going to pass this year and there's my self-confidence completely shattered.

In general, how do you feel at the moment about being dyslexic?

Kind of disappointed. I'm doing really badly at university and I'm failing quite badly, I've had a lot of work to do. If I wasn't dyslexic maybe I might have been better off, maybe I would have done better in the assignments, better in the exams. If it hadn't happened it would have been fantastic, to be like everyone else.

Comment

Patrick reports that he was quiet and withdrawn early on in school. This is a common response of children having difficulty in learning to read and write. He also says that he was described as a loner, which relates to the issue discussed in Chapter 1 of whether such children are at greater risk of social isolation because of deficits in their underlying processing skills or whether this is entirely a secondary outcome of their low self-esteem and withdrawal from social interactions. Fisher, Allen and Kose (1996) have suggested that the critical factor may be the level of anxiety; high anxiety may impair children's performance and lead to social withdrawal.

Interestingly, at secondary school, Patrick talks about having friends in higher academic groups, which seems to suggest that his underlying intelligence and good verbal skills were recognised by his peers. By contrast, Patrick felt that the message he received from his teachers was that he was stupid. In addition, he felt that his parents, although concerned for him, accepted the school's view of him. Even after he was identified as dyslexic he appears to have received minimal support from his family or professionals in understanding what dyslexia entails and how best to cope with it. Many successful adults with dyslexia emphasise that the support of their family was critical in enabling them to succeed. As Patrick points out, his family should not be blamed for not knowing about dyslexia and he feels that his teachers, as professionals, should take the major responsibility.

In listening to Patrick's interview one gets an immediate impression that here is someone in trouble who is struggling badly with his course. Patrick himself is unsure how far these difficulties should be attributed to dyslexia alone. This kind of study cannot answer this question, but in conjunction with the wider literature it does suggest that dyslexia may be an additional risk factor, which increases the chances of some students running into difficulties. Patrick has received little support for either his literacy difficulties or his secondary problems of low self-esteem and anxiety, and he was obviously in urgent need of help. Although Patrick works hard, the negative feedback that he receives is further undermining his confidence, and this appears to have led to a vicious downward spiral, with his anxiety increasing as he does less work and, in turn, his further anxiety about falling behind leading to sleeplessness and an impaired ability to cope with his work. By default this has led to the adoption of negative strategies such as missing lectures, which have resulted in even more anxiety. When the factors that are identified as leading to success are:

1. A supportive environment,
2. Developing positive coping strategies,
3. Persistence,
4. Drawing on support networks,

it is hardly surprising that Patrick, with his lack of support, is experiencing difficulties. Although Patrick has an awareness of his difficulties and appears to be trying to develop some coping strategies, his anxiety appears to be impairing this process and he displays many of the features of learned helplessness. This is a state where someone feels that nothing they do will make the situation better and is often the result of long experience in a no-win situation. In addition, Patrick doesn't seem to feel entitled to help and seems to blame himself for his difficulties at university.

Research into attribution style suggests that people vary consistently in how far they 'blame' themselves or 'blame' other people or circumstances when they encounter difficulties, and this may be an important factor in how individuals cope with dyslexia but more systematic research is needed before anything more definite can be said. Being prepared to work harder than other students and to ask for help is sometimes presented as if it were an unproblematic solution to literacy difficulties. But, like many of the students in this sample, Patrick was ashamed of his written work and did not want others to see it and therefore did not ask for help with tasks like proofreading his work. In addition, he still seemed to link the need for extra work with the feeling that he was less able than other students, even though at an intellectual level he knew he was as intelligent. This may be an important area for some students to resolve, and it is important that support for these kinds of worry is available. It can be argued that successful students probably reframe the experience of having to work harder as a positive coping strategy and as a way of achieving their goals and demonstrating that they can do as well as other students. It should also be pointed out that Patrick received one of the highest spelling-error scores on the free-writing task and, like Andy, presented as one of the most severely dyslexic students in the sample. They both seem to have the same risk factors of lack of early identification, lack of family support and a high degree of severity, and it is perhaps no coincidence that they have both suffered from mental health problems.

Chapter 10
Jenny

'this is the dyslexic who all along covered up and this is why they've never found out'

Jenny attended a private school where the academic emphasis was very strong. Her parents were very supportive, but she covered up her difficulties and suffered in silence for most of her school career. She emerged with 3 'A' levels and entered university straight away to follow a social sciences course. Her Adult Dyslexia Checklist score is very high and her self-esteem rating is low.

The Interview

Could you specify what kinds of difficulty you had at school?

Well, reading has been a big problem, tracking from getting to the end of one line to the beginning of the next. How I found out I was dyslexic was from my music teacher, because I was jumping notes and I was going from the end of the line to the next – so that's how I found out. I had extra English lessons right from the age of 11 at school, but that was just for spelling, I never ever considered that it was dyslexia.

Did your teachers recognise that you had any difficulties at all?

At age 15, at Easter just before my GCSEs, it was my music teacher. My English teacher just said I had terrible spelling and terrible grammar, but never said it was anything to do with dyslexia and I had extra English lessons to teach me spelling.

Who was the first person to identify your dyslexia?

That was the Dyslexic Institute at Staines, who said I was dyslexic but didn't give any guidance after that. I then had lessons from a lady who took me through the spelling rules. It wasn't anybody that the Staines Institute had sent.

Did your parents recognise that you had difficulties?

They knew right from the start about spelling – right from the age of primary school at about 6. They talked to the teachers all the time and they said 'it'll come'. So they weren't bothered at all. Then at school I had extra English – my teachers giving extra English.

Did that extra English help at all?

It's sort of demoralising, teaching spelling that a 5 year old should know ... There's also stigma with your friends of [your] going to extra English ... Baby spellings, I just went through basic spellings, I learnt parrot fashion, but when it came to actually writing, I didn't know them. But that was a vicious circle because that was time taken out of lessons, time taken to do exercises, which put me at a disadvantage against everyone else, because I was missing work time. Then you had to catch up, which was a vicious circle. My parents [gave me] extra lessons, extra note-taking and re-learning spellings, which helped.

Were you formally assessed as being dyslexic, and was this recognised at your school?

Their reaction really was, 'There's no such thing'. My class teacher said that when she was taught how to teach she was told there is no such thing.

Was that the opinion of most of the teachers at the school?

Yes it was. 'If you've been diagnosed as being dyslexic you can't possibly be.' And they didn't really acknowledge it at all. And I had extra time, but that wasn't acknowledged and I had real trouble getting extra time.

This extra time, was it after school?

No, it was in exams. They never really told my teachers about this, I think it was written down on records but never referred to at all, but they never did anything about it.

Before the assessment, what did you think of yourself and why did you think you were having difficulties? Did you think you were slow?

Right at the beginning from when I was about 5 or 6 at school we had maths and English books that we had to work through as a class, sort of informal, and when you were stuck you had to ask the teacher. I knew at that point I was slow because I gradually got behind and that was a vicious circle, because the more I got behind I didn't want to go and ask the teachers for help. So I slipped back so I could do the work. I was very slow, once I'd done the practical work, at actually writing it up. I could do chemistry, whereas I hated write-ups. That was right from an early age, and I was absolutely terrified of spelling tests, and the humiliation you get from the teacher saying 'you haven't learnt them'. And you know you'd spent the whole evening trying to learn them – and you're friends picking on you.

So did you have a sort of negative image of yourself?

It's kind of negative, but that's looking back now, because I didn't know at the time that I had a problem. That's something I knew but my parents hadn't really picked up on it, and I didn't know it was something different.

And the responses that the teachers have given you?

I just thought it was me being slow and not knowing. My brother's at the same school and he was very slow and he got picked on a lot by the teacher and you think it's you being slow and you don't want to make an issue of it ... It becomes like a self-fulfilling prophecy, the teachers saying 'you must be stupid' and 'you're very slow', so you think you must be because the teacher's saying so ... By saying that and you know you're learning it the night before, you think you're even more stupid, putting hours into it and still getting a bad mark.

You can see what a tremendous hurdle you've overcome to get here today at the university, any dyslexic student that makes that deserves a gold star.

It was kind of negative because all the way through I was told not to do this GCSE and not to do this, that and the other, not because I was dyslexic, but because I was slow and incapable.

How did you overcome that – the teacher saying you can't do that qualification? I suppose you have to believe?

Well I just did it in the end. But the strange thing was that they made me do English because the whole year did English Language early and they made me do English Language early, even though I was having extra English lessons. They made me do that early even though I didn't want to. They put me down to do it.

There's a lot of determination there.

Well there had to be, the whole time you're fighting against the teachers who say that you can't do things and that you're lazy. English Language I got second time around.

How was maths?

I got a 'B' in maths; I've always enjoyed maths, I like geometry, that side of maths, that's always OK.

Did knowing that you were dyslexic change the way you saw yourself and did this have an effect on your academic work or relationships with other people? Were you nervous of meeting other people?

I remember because I had been down to Staines [Dyslexia Institute], because I was at boarding school. I remember coming back Sunday evening. My parents took me down there and I didn't really know what the Institute was. I'd never heard of dyslexia before. And my music teacher talked to my mother and they sort of organised it between them. So I went down there not knowing what was going to happen – doing all these tests and being told that you're dyslexic and thinking it's some kind of disease. I was sort of put in there. This is it – they've come out with a label.

What was your knowledge of dyslexia before you were assessed?

Nothing, when I first knew I remember sitting in the waiting room and looking round seeing all these people who were dyslexic and thought: 'Oh gosh, I'm here – all these quotes from people and illustrations of children writing.'

How did yu feel after the assessment?

After sort of coming out of the centre and you look at the assessment and think: 'Oh look, I am dyslexic'. It makes everything fall into place and you think 'That's why' and you analyse everything afterwards. When you're writing you analyse how you are writing, and it's sort of a weight off my mind. But then you've got this label and you have to deal with it and think 'I've got to overcome this thing'. In a way I'm quite pleased I hadn't known until I was 15, because if I'd known earlier it might have been an excuse, or there would have been a reason for not doing your GCSEs.

So you're mature enough?

Yes, because you have dealt with it in the past so you can go on dealing with it, as you said earlier. I think also the teachers might have said 'Oh you can't do this', and you probably would have listened to them. In a way I was quite glad I didn't know. I've learnt to cope now because now you can't keep saying to everyone you're dyslexic, you have to come to terms with it.

Did you receive support for your dyslexia from the centre afterwards?

I didn't think that they were that helpful.

So there weren't regular times to go along?

I had the assessment, but the backup after that was non-existent. And I thought: 'They told me this terrible thing' and that I'd walked out with this saying, 'You're dyslexic'. I felt there was this sort of stigma after that, telling friends. It was really strange, it was like saying 'I've got this illness' and they hadn't come across it.

Were your friends aware of what dyslexia was?

Yes, I think some of them were, but I certainly wasn't.

You received very little support in terms of building up your spelling skills and structuring...?

That was outside school, it was 2 hours outside school time.

Did the school notice any change after going to this lady?

No, they didn't really know. They did know but they didn't really take it in that's what I was doing, something I was doing, and they weren't prepared to help at all.

Was it a grammar school you went to?

No, it was a boarding school. I think they thought it was more of a stigma and they didn't want to acknowledge anyone who was [dyslexic], what I did find I was always much slower and in the lower sets, especially with languages. I found those really difficult. I'd gone into school being really good at French and I got there and I just went right down and I stayed, I found languages very difficult. In the assessment my IQ came out OK, which was nice for me to know as I was much slower than everyone else.

In general, do you feel that your family have been supportive or unsupportive in dealing with your dyslexia?

Very supportive.

Yes, I remember earlier you said your parents had spotted there was a problem.

Yes, they thought it should have been the teachers, but they had to take it on themselves.

So they were responsible for the assessment.

The school didn't do anything.

What was the reaction from your parents to the school after that?

Not good, because school, really, they only concentrated on the Oxbridge-type person, if you had anything slightly different, my brother found this as well, they didn't want to know, they were only concentrating on the people that did their 'A' [level]s.

So it was a case of your family being the supportive ones and the education system failing.

Yes, I mean the careers education after that was non-existent and I had to do all the careers stuff myself. My parents helped me as well, the school didn't help at all, especially when you were going to a poly[technic college] as opposed to a university, no support at all.

So turning to the present, do you think that the sort of problems that you face at university are much the same as other students'? What problems are particular to you?

Reading – which has been all the way along. I managed to pass my English Literature without reading the end of any book.... At school if they said 'read this chapter then we'll discuss it', I would never ever get anywhere near halfway through it, so I'd miss out on the discussion. And I'm still the same now, it's trying to read quickly and taking in what I'm reading. I can read a page and not actually take in what I've read, or I can read and skim out odd words that I need and find that I haven't actually taken anything in. If I want to read and take anything in it takes a long time and I sort of stop and highlight something or underline it really.

Basically the difference from other students is having to read the script two or three times before it'll all go in?

Yes, a lot, and I sort of think I didn't know all that and couldn't tell you anything about it.

When you are reading the text do the words appear to move, or is it a problem focusing on them?

It's a problem refocusing on them, getting from one line to the next, and also when taking notes from the blackboard, it's writing it down and going back to the board to try and find where I was – that's a difficulty. So I have never read a book for pleasure. Spelling – when I'm writing an essay I'll spell one word differently the whole way through the essay. I just spell it how I say it. It's really embarrassing. I hate writing by hand in front of people. Like writing cheques – I hate writing cheques, I don't know how to write the numbers. Well, I couldn't say if I've written the numbers right or wrong, just spellings ... it's sort of an embarrassment when someone's watching you.

In what way, if any, do you think dyslexia is affecting your academic work? Do you have to contribute in tutorials? How do you feel about speaking in public for instance?

I don't really like doing that. It's got a lot better. In our course we have to do a lot of presentations and are marked on them. But I found reading things out I'd stumble over words. At school you have to read out a passage and this always terrified me because, you know, going from one line to the next, I'd stumble on words. I wouldn't recognise a word, say it wrong and just sort of try to say things. I noticed this with my brother as well. It sounds like his brain's going faster than his mouth. He stumbles over words, and I don't like having to speak out like that because I think it's going to come out completely wrong so that puts me off saying things. That's improved – it's just something I've always avoided. At school, we were meant to do readings in assembly, but I never did it at all at school. I always managed to get out of it. It was just the sort of nervousness of getting it wrong, stumbling.

And that's a difficulty that's persisted right up until now in tutorials and seminars?

When I was doing revision for GCSEs I worked with somebody else and spoke everything and I learnt it a lot better doing it that way than writing notes down – from actually chatting about a subject ...Writing notes down from the board is very slow ... I found it difficult to try to take in what they're saying and write down at the same time. I find that very difficult.

You find that you have to take them home and read them again and again?

If you can look at that with someone else I find that a real benefit and that got me through my GCSEs, actually talking through everything with somebody else.

Have you told any of your tutors about being dyslexic at all?

Yes, at the end of last term, I wasn't actually going to tell them at all, but I thought after 'A' levels ... From that experience ... I thought I wouldn't tell anybody because I couldn't see an advantage of saying it and I thought 'I'll see if I can get through without telling them'.

What was their response?

Well, my course leader has been really good about it and was saying 'of course you'll need extra time in exams', and he was positive in saying that most dyslexic people have high IQs. I was really worried about prejudices against marking my work, that was my real concern. I sort of thought now by the third year they would know that I'm dyslexic.

Did any tutors or lecturers pick up on spelling mistakes through the two years?

Yes, I've had essays back where the comment has been 'bad spelling' and I thought 'oh no, maybe I should have told them'.

How about writing letters to friends; if you're handwriting a letter to a friend, how do you feel?

What I actually do now, because I hate writing anything like that, I do that on the word processor. I spellcheck it then I write it out by hand. And it's trying to get the flow of conversation going and trying to use words that you know you can spell and trying to write as well, because I do find that I use words that I know that are right or I think are right.

So, in some sense, you could be avoiding words that you can't spell; you sort of just wouldn't put it in, for example, 'beautifully'?

I find I do that a lot, you actually don't know whether it's right or wrong and I just don't have any concepts of that. Sometimes I can – it just depends. Sometimes [with] really small words, I have no idea how to begin to write the word, which is a problem when taking down notes. You just get stuck.

Do you get funding from the LEA [local education authority] and how are you using it, have you applied for the disabled students' allowance [DSA]?

Yes, I applied for the computer and that hasn't come through yet. But I never heard [of the DSA] till last term.

So you hadn't heard about the disabled students' allowance until last term?

I've got this computer and I'm applying for it now and it's just amazing. I can write fluently on the computer and I just type it in. Whereas if I was doing it by hand I would have a problem, because I could never do the first sentence, I just sort of get permanently [stuck] on the first page, which is sort of a real problem and that goes back to when I was about 8 or 9 and my mother used to say 'write something on the page' and I just used to be stuck.

Did you have any difficulties with the LEA?

They've been OK about it, sort of relaxed.

What strategies have you found effective in helping you deal with your work?

Spending extra time.

What about other things that you do differently from other students?

I don't know really, because I do things subconsciously like writing other words that I know I can spell better, that's really trying to avoid it – because this is the dyslexic who all along covered up and this is why they've never found out, because I've covered it up all the time right from an early age. And it wasn't so bad that it was obvious, just by covering up and using different words and getting out of things.

In a way that's a sort of strategy in itself.

It is sort of getting out of doing things in front of the class like having to write on the board or having to read out aloud, and then there's having to do with extra spelling tests.

So you're using technology at the moment on the computer; have you got a grammar check?

Yes.

Do you find that the spellchecker picks up on the kind of mistakes you might be making on the computer?

Yes it does pick up, but this is only recently that I've found out from a friend if you have spelt some words wrong like 'fourth' and it's 'f.o.r.', there's another one and it doesn't pick up on that and I never really thought about that.

Do you think knowing that you are dyslexic affects your confidence in your ability to do academic work?

It's been sort of negative and positive: negative, I think, because I'm sort of held back from doing certain things; like in class I've never got up and done presentations, which is good now because they've made me [do it] on my course and I would never have done it. I would always get out of things. And I think positively, it's really made me do more than what I would have otherwise done. And if I had my teacher's way right from the age of 8 he said that I probably wouldn't do any 'A' levels, and in the secondary [school] they said give up GCSEs and do one 'A' level and then you'll never get into university.

So it has made you more determined.

Yes, it does feel as if I have succeeded.

And then you've conquered that hurdle, and it does seem like a big hurdle to conquer, that you could probably conquer most things.

I've sort of achieved things that people who are perfectly normal find difficult.

How do you think that your particular personality influences the way you deal with your dyslexia or, conversely, has having dyslexia had an influence on your personality?

I've never really wanted to say anything to teachers. I've not really liked going up and making excuses. No, I'd rather suffer in silence than go and say anything.

Does having dyslexia affect your general self-esteem?

Yes, because you sort of think you've got this high level of IQ and think: 'If I hadn't got this dyslexia what could I have done?' It's frustrating, because you want to do things and you know you're being held back by dyslexia – that is really frustrating. You see the other people who you went to school with and think 'Could I have done that?', and then you come back and sort of think: 'Well, I have done this and they only thought I could do that', so it works in two ways.

Do you tell other students that you are dyslexic here at the university?

Only very recently, and just a few. I mean I've been living with my flatmates for most of my second year and I have only told one of them. One of them I went to school with and the others I didn't really know. Until a few days ago – it just came out and I decided to say something.

What was the sort of reception you got?

She [flatmate] didn't believe it because she's doing Engineering and she's always saying, 'You know there are so many dyslexic people doing Engineering and I hate getting in a group with them because they can't write.' And I'm just sitting there thinking ... And I just said: 'Oh, actually ...' and she couldn't believe it.

So she didn't see any indication in the house?

We had this board for leaving messages and I hate leaving messages on this board. Apart from that, she wouldn't have noticed. One of the girls did know.

How did you feel after you said it?

I don't get frustrated because I knew what she'd been saying – or sort of – last year. I don't think she'd ever come across it, but her attitude was 'they can't spell' and everyone hopes that they don't get into a group with them, because they can't spell and you can't read what they've written.

So you were faced with a prejudiced situation.

Yes, sort of saying 'One of them wears these coloured glasses and they said "oh it's something to do with dyslexia" and I didn't believe them', and I said: 'Well actually that is true'.

Do you ever ask other students or staff for specific help?

Well actually for 'A' level Economics I sat next to a girl who was really helpful, because I always got behind taking down notes so when there was a pause, well, when the teacher was actually talking and not putting notes up, I would just copy off her notes and she would just help me that way, so I got help getting through the notes and people lending me their notes. I only told certain people and I didn't really want to.

Do you find it embarrassing to talk about dyslexia?

It depends, sometimes I find it embarrassing, but other times I think, you know, sort of proving that you can go to university, like my flatmate and she didn't know.

Are there any situations that you find particularly difficult or embarrassing because of your dyslexia, sort of in everyday life, like writing cheques, which you mentioned before, or timetables?

I never could do tables. That's another thing – at school they used to point at you and say ... and learning chemistry formulas. I passed a Chemistry 'C' without knowing any formulas apart from only one. It's something I could not do myself. If I was concentrating on anything else I forgot the formulas. That was just impossible because I was there on a Saturday morning having to do retests for chemistry, knowing that I had spent more time trying to learn than other people who would just look at it a few minutes before.

Have you ever felt isolated at university or when you were younger because of your dyslexia?

Well, everybody thinks that you're different, but you just don't know what to do about it.

Was that more so at school?

School, not now because I've never really talked about it. It's only been since I went to the talk last term that I have ever actually talked about it at university, otherwise you just sort of forget about it and just carry on. I just made this decision to go to university and forget about it.

Is it comforting when you meet another dyslexic person?

Yes, it is nice, because you do feel completely isolated, as if you are fighting this lone battle.

Especially with the experience you had at school.

It's no wonder when you end up at university, you think, 'Well, I'm going to fight you all on my own' ...Well I hated school because of that. Looking back, school was a struggle all the time, and everyone looks back at school and says: 'Oh she didn't used to do any work.' And I think: 'Oh, gosh ... I feel I spent all that time having to work.' And for everyone else it's a minor part, they can go off and do other things, and I was there learning how to spell.

So you would find it helpful to meet other dyslexic students?

I think that the main benefit would be to talk to others ... I think you learn quite a lot about coping strategies and how to deal with it ... Better than having to do lessons and relearning how to do some things – it is still demoralising. But it's learning to cope at the level you are now, [it is] sort of an ongoing process.

Have you met anyone in the past or now who has ridiculed your dyslexia? I suppose we covered that with the housemates. Have you ever come across that sort of stigma with teachers basically?

Nobody else, friends of mine have been positive. It was just the teacher who literally turned around and said: 'Well basically I was taught that there was no such thing', and that was the end of that. And I didn't know what to believe then – conflicting arguments. And I used to think: 'Well look, I am normal and I'm not being lazy.' Then you start to think, 'Am I being stupid?'

In general, how do you feel at the moment about being dyslexic, do you think you're happier being dyslexic?

I don't know. I mean it's had its benefits. I mean I probably wouldn't have ever thought about what I'd been doing if I hadn't been dyslexic – I analyse a lot – and it is something you've had to sort of fight and you can succeed against.

So it has been a challenge?

Yes, it has been a challenge and for me I want to go back to my teacher and say I've got that 'A' level and you told me I was going to fail it. It would be nice to be recognised [as dyslexic] – that's the worst thing to me – to not be able to be recognised [as dyslexic] when you've done something wrong – and that's the worst thing really, because it's embarrassing for you. When you are at home and you're writing an essay, then you're on your own and you can spellcheck things. It's when you're face to face and they say to you 'Write this down' and you think 'Oh gosh' – it sort of distracts from what you're actually writing. There are other people out there who have got an advantage and employers would much rather have them than you, you can't even spell.

Is there anything that I haven't raised that you would like to talk about?

Just bringing it back – the first 2 years at university, I've never really thought about it.

This is the first time that you have sat down and talked about it?

Yes, I've never actually talked to anyone about it – apart from with friends, I've never really talked about it.

Comment

Personality and coping

Jenny's account of her years at school and her struggles with her difficulty give the impression of a fairly self-contained and determined personality. Before she was identified as dyslexic she appears to have been motivated to achieve and to do well at school despite her difficulties. She internalised her struggles, and a theme that emerges continually in Jenny's interview is her feeling that she should suffer in silence, 'You can't keep saying to everyone you're dyslexic, you have to come to terms with it.' Although her parents identified her difficulties at an early age, her school experience was that there was no recognition of her specific difficulties and that she had to find ways of covering up her problems and coping despite them. But she says, 'In a way, I'm quite glad that I didn't know until I was 15, because if I'd known earlier it might have been an excuse – or there would have been a reason for not doing GCSEs.' Jenny frequently mentions the amount of work she did outside school hours and how little this paid off in school. She expresses her frustration with the fact that her work was not acknowledged and, indeed, everyone considered that she was lazy. She would learn and relearn spellings, tables and chemistry formulas – but when it came to the test, she could not remember them. A major coping strategy was the avoidance of situations in which she knew she would fail – such as reading aloud in assembly and avoiding writing words that she is unsure how to spell.

Peer support

A way of coping that Jenny found most helpful was getting a little help from her friends and peers: someone who let her copy their notes in her 'A'-level Economics class; a friend who worked with her on GCSEs, with whom she was able to chat about the subjects. Her reticence is very evident, however, when she says: 'I only told certain people and I didn't really want to.' There is ample evidence that peer support in learning situations can be a very effective aid (Gardner, 1987). In addition, good relationships in the learning situation are important for most young learners. The links and interactions between cognitive and emotional development are still unclear. But we are certain that too much stress in the learning situation interferes with learning (Gentile and McMillan, 1987).

Coping at university

Jenny's strategies have, in the past, been largely concerned with covering up her difficulties by avoiding situations in which they would be highlighted. But recently she has discovered the delights of a word processor. 'I've got this computer and ... it's just amazing. I can write fluently on the computer. I just type it in.'

Still reluctant to trust others and to tell them of her problems, Jenny feels that she would benefit from talking to other dyslexic students. She is aware that she needs to develop coping strategies to deal with the level of learning and the type of study required of her.

Severity – type of dyslexia

Jenny's problems were evidently not so much in the area of learning to read but with written work, spelling, copying from the blackboard, taking notes, and rate of work. Reading difficulties are evident, however, when she discusses her problems of skipping lines, omitting words, having to read and reread passages in order to take in the meaning. She has difficulties with everyday activities such as writing notes for her friends, writing cheques and writing letters by hand. She has difficulty in speaking to groups, in ordering her words to say what she means. Her problems were not picked up early on in her school career because of this mixture of abilities and disabilities, and her writing and other difficulties were attributed to stupidity and laziness rather than to a learning difficulty.

Coping with the label

Jenny is quite ambivalent about being labelled dyslexic and acknowledging her difficulties. Her first understanding was that it was some kind of disease that she had contracted in some way, which was incurable. She relates that she felt there would be a sort of stigma attached to it after that when, and if, she told her friends. 'It was really strange, it was like saying "I've got this illness" and they hadn't come across it.' The positive aspect of the label is that it makes everything fall into place and she begins to understand why school has been such a struggle for her. She says: 'It's a sort of weight off my mind.' Then she acknowledges that after the initial dawning of understanding of her past came the awareness that she has to deal with it and she has to 'overcome this thing'. She regards it as a challenge that she is determined to confront, despite other people's attitudes.

The public declaration of the label has had many negative effects for Jenny. Initially, at 15, when she was diagnosed as dyslexic, she remembers her teachers' reactions as being 'There's no such thing'. She had trouble getting extra time in exams, which was her right. On reaching university, therefore, on the basis of her 'A' level experience, she decides that she will not tell anybody because she cannot see any advantage in doing so. She receives essays marked with the comment 'bad spelling' and finally decides to tell her tutors – but she remains concerned that there will be prejudice against her work. Jenny's fears of the prejudicial effects that the label can have on others is borne out in the conversation she has with her flatmate, who states that she hates being in a group with dyslexics because they cannot spell and you cannot read what they have written. She remain wary of the label and its effects, and later states that other people out there have an advantage: 'employers would much rather have them than you – you can't even spell'.

Chapter 11
Henry

'I constantly weigh up its good and bad points...At school I used to be [bothered by dyslexia]...Nowadays I'm almost proud of it.'

Henry is a 25-year-old student doing a degree in Electronic Engineering. His score on the Adult Dyslexia Checklist indicates a problem of intermediate severity. His spelling is consistent with this. His interview is consistent with his psychometric scores for self-esteem, trait and state anxiety, all of which fall within the range of normal variation.

The Interview

Do you think the experiences you had before coming to university are affecting the way you are coping now?

I didn't think I was [dyslexic]. I didn't think I had any problems actually. It was my mother who thought I had and so I got assessed when I was 9, which was quite early, especially in those days. Then it came back I was [dyslexic]. I really did not think that I had a problem with my English although in retrospect... Then I went to a private school. Instead of moving on to secondary school I went to a private school because the secondary school did not recognise dyslexia and I would have just gone into their remedial sets. So I went to the private school and there wasn't any main problem, apart from reading out loud in the class. You're waiting for your turn and you don't want to do it. But I didn't usually have to do it with the main English teacher, but when people stood in for them they used to make me read, which I didn't like. From there I went to another private school which I didn't really like very much, and I left there to go to a comprehensive school, and there I didn't read [out loud]. I was asked to [but] I refused.

Did the teachers recognise that you had any difficulties?

I think that any teacher who read any of my writing realised that there was a bit of a problem. I think that dyslexia is far deeper than just problems with English. Not being good at reading and writing [is] merely a symptom of a more complicated thing. People call it word blindness. I don't think that's right at all. It's a learning difficulty. I don't think it's tied to English at all.

Did any teacher at secondary school recognise that you had any difficulties?

They [had] all been told about it. It was quite a new thing, which made me quite hip. They would say 'Look Henry, I know you have this problem'. They did recognise it.

Did they give any support?

No, they did not give me any support or help. They just said that we know you are a bit crap at it, rather than bending over backwards to approach things from a different angle.

Did your parents recognise that you had difficulties?

Yes they did.

Before you were assessed, what did you think of yourself, and why did you think you were having difficulties?

No, not at all, but if I'd been asked to sit down and think about it and [asked] 'Out of all your subjects which subjects are you particularly bad in?', I would have said English. This is something I'm quite bad at [but] it didn't show up as a big difficulty. When my mother said it was [dyslexia] I was not sure whether to believe her or not. She said that I would need extra lessons and I said 'But why?' I thought my writing was fine.

Did any of the teachers at school accuse you of being lazy at all?

No, not really, because I was the famous one. A famous dyslexic, because it was found out early on. So everyone cottoned on to it and recognised it. But not recognise as in sort of help you or teach you differently. They just said, ' It's OK, we understand you're not thick, it's because you've got a problem'.

Did knowing that you were dyslexic change the way you saw yourself and did this have any effect on your academic work or relationships with other people?

I use to get frustrated that other people used to understand things that I couldn't understand, like maths and things. I was so frustrated that I couldn't get it. Then I realised that they did not actually understand it. That's what helped my frustration a bit, realising that I wanted to understand things more deeply than other people.

Did you receive any additional help and support for your dyslexia? Do you think it helped you?

At the private school this woman used to come in and teach me things. I don't think that really helped, and I went to the Dyslexia Institute and I don't really think that helped either, to be honest. If you want to read then you should lock yourself in a room with a book and practise it for a lot of time. It's not worth learning all the rules – the spelling rules. It's not a scientific thing. It is an art. For instance, if you want to draw a car you'll sit down and [practise] drawing loads of cars. It's no good saying, 'Oh, the windscreen is always tilted at some degree and the wheels are always round'. You've just got to practise drawing them.

What would you say your specific difficulties were then?

Specific difficulty was spelling. I'd spell things phonetically instead of how they should have been and I still don't see that as a difficulty. Language has been evolving and changing with what is best, but now it has stopped evolving and changing because everyone has tied down the rules and [been] teaching people specific words. So, unfortunately, through evolution we can't get rid of stupid words. We will always have 'k' on the front of 'knife'. In the old days nobody would have bothered putting the 'k' in front. There is no reason for it all – n.i.f.e. would do perfectly. It wouldn't clash with other words. My biggest problem was getting ' b's and ' d's round the wrong way and things like that.

Do these types of error still occur today?

Oh yes. I got a ' b' wrong yesterday. Only the little ones.

You still spell words phonetically?

Yes, I do. But it's OK because you can hit a non-dyslexic with a phonetic word and they can read it, but it's just when you hit a dyslexic with a normal word, [an] irregular word, he would be knackered, whereas if the dyslexic spells it phonetically he can understand it.

So you received additional help right up until the age of...?

I had this woman coming in to see me at primary school and then I got lessons from the Dyslexia Institute. Then I took my entrance exams for the private school but they said that I'd have to improve on my English. So they accepted me on the basis that I attended the Dyslexia Institute. I remember at the time that it was not an enlightening experience, but if you did look at my work before and after it probably did improve. It didn't feel like any great relief. It wasn't the answer.

While you were in post-16 education, how did you cope with your academic work?

I did an apprenticeship. I didn't do any 'A' levels or anything like that. I did a foundation year.

In general, do you feel that your family have been supportive or unsupportive to you in dealing with your dyslexia?

Well my mother set up a dyslexia institute, so, yes, very much so.

Is there anyone else in the family who has dyslexia?

Yes, my younger sister and probably my dad, even though it's an unmentioned thing. My dad shows all the signs although he has never been assessed and never would be either. But he does show the signs of it, and my little sister is as well.

What are the indicating signs?

She was bad at English too and my older sister is partially dyslexic. She is an arty type and she wanted to enter this competition in London for dyslexics. It was nice to know that other people are dyslexic, but I was severely dyslexic at the time and in comparison to my sisters. It took me ages to get the 'b's and 'd's. I was all over the place.

Is there a similarity between the types of error that you and your sister make?

I'm not sure really. She was more to do with spelling. She was quite neat at her handwriting. My handwriting wasn't that good. When I'm trying to write a sentence I get to a full stop and there is more stuff to put in before my full stop. It's more of a structuring problem than a specific spelling or reading [problem]. I've always been all right with reading but I never read for fun. I just cannot read for fun. I can read instructions. Instructions are great. In one sentence you can get two or three juicy facts. You get far more from it. When you get a novel you might need to read a 100 words just to describe the sky. You're, like, reading through it and concentrating on the page. You don't get enough back for the amount you put in. So I've never read for fun. I've only ever read two books.

When you read a book do you find the words appear to move?

No, I don't get that. I don't think that's classified as dyslexia. It sounds like a cornea or retina problem.

How about your comprehension of a text?

I [am] always too exact. I sometimes find things difficult to understand when I'm reading them, I can't ask [the book] questions. 'What do you mean it's big'? It's like saying such and such is very big, and I am saying, like, '"Big" – what exactly does it mean'? People say that I'm splitting hairs, but I'm not. I'm not being awkward. I just see things in a different light.

So, in summing up, you didn't have any particular problems with the teachers?

I use to cry when I didn't understand things. I used to get so frustrated. It really used to do my head in, a big lump in my throat. As soon as you're frustrated you're not going to take anything in, are you?

How about reading out loud in class?

If I knew I had to read [in class] I would read and memorise the first line and think, 'Right, what I'm going to do [is] I'll read this first line out and some magic will enable me to fly through it all'. I would read the first line as quick as possible to compensate for the slowness of the rest of it, then I'd get totally knackered. I remember in secondary school we all had to read out a part in a play and the teacher said, 'Henry, you can be the policemen' and he only had one word to say, and the point was, what the hell did this word say? I would stare at this word and it was 'quite', and I kept looking at it and I said 'quit' instead of 'quite'. It was so embarrassing, like. I just stopped doing it after then.

Why did you choose to study at the university?

The course, Electrical and Electronic Engineering.

Was your dyslexia an issue when applying to university?

I was contemplating doing a Law degree before I chose Electronics. I was into electronics then but I thought law would be more interesting, but I decided, because of the reading and writing involved, I thought, that is not suited for me. Dyslexia was an issue when deciding what degree to do. I wouldn't say, 'Look I'm dyslexic', but if I want to do law I should be able to just go in and say, ' Look I want to do law, and you lot are going to have to give me extra help'. I'm not really suited to that. I wouldn't want to be a sprinter if I only had one leg, except for the fact that I'm not that good at running.

So, turning to the present, do you think that the sorts of problem that you face at university are much the same as other students'?

No. With my course it's an understanding problem and I need to understand the things, and the problem being that, with a lot of the courses, especially physics, it's just not understood. I mean, we've got the equations to prove it, though even most of the lecturers aren't really sure about what is really going on. So a lot of people pass their exams although they have not really got a clue what they are doing. There are a lot of subjects where I know what I'm doing yet I can't pass exams. I've got an understanding problem. I want to get into things more deeply but I just get the answer, ' Oh sorry, that's not on the syllabus'. I need to understand this bit before I go on to the next bit. I'm good at understanding things but I need to know all the information. There is a lot of assumptions that go on. They're all hidden away behind this front end that we're concentrating on, and I show them all up.

Do you have any problems with deadlines?

No.

Any other problems at all?

Sometimes with the labs. When you've got to do the labs you're trying to get over a simple point, and I do it and then I get really confused and frustrated in the labs. I can see what they're on about but I can't fully see how it works, but when I get home it all seems obvious. When I'm put on the spot, I can't do it. I think that's dyslexia.

How about seminars?

I am good at them. I'm good at communication and talking. That compensates for my lack of reading and writing work.

How about written assignments?

Well, I'll just write them on the computer and spellcheck it.

How would you cope without a word processor?

I don't put an importance on spelling like everyone else does. I really don't care about it really, a lot of it is redundant.

Have you told any of your tutors about your difficulties?

Yes, I've got a problem because my personal tutor is Head of the Department, so any problem you have he takes it as a personal criticism about how he is running his department. I prefer to be [known as] dyslexic than not. Although my spelling is very poor, people do know what you're going on about.

What was your tutor's response?

There was one lecturer the other week and he tried to make a fool out of me. Again he thought I was being pedantic. He was doing a system control, that was his subject, and his first overhead said 'system control' but he spelt system with an 'n' so to me it read 'systen' and I thought that should be an 'm', and that's , like, a lavatory cistern. So I said that should be spelt with an 'm' not an 'n', but he replied '"cistern" begins with a "c", not an "s"', and he said, 'Oh I remember you', and then later on he was talking about something else and it was a long word and he said, 'I'll just write that on the board for people who can't spell'.

Are you currently receiving support for your dyslexia?

No, I'm not receiving help from the university. I did get a personal computer from the council. But I was offered extra time in the exams, or rather I was asked if I wanted to apply for that, but I didn't.

Do you get any funding from the LEA [local education authority]?

Yes, I got the grant for the personal computer.

Did you find that useful?

Oh yes, very, because it can handle the spelling. I really don't see why people put this great importance on spelling – as long as you can see what it says.

Ideally, what sort of support should be available for dyslexic students?

I think that it shouldn't be like that. They should go to their own university and [be] taught in different ways. Everyone thinks of it as a disability and a problem, but I don't think like that at all. I think that you've got the potential to achieve things that a normal person never could and to come out with new things and have a deeper understanding, far deeper than any normal person could. So, rather than trying to make dyslexic people fit into a normal one [university] and bringing them down to that level, I think they should look at the whole subject in a different way and teach in a different way and you would get higher achievers. Although it sounds big-headed, because it is told to me the other way round, you've got to always fit into the way other people do it. It's a bit big-headed for normal people to think that their way is best.

So what aspects of your work do you do well in?

I think practical and intuition, inventing things, and coming up with ideas. I [am] quite good with them, but I'm no good at dishing out rubbish for the sake of it. If it is meaningless to me then it is very, very difficult to understand. I really can't remember the [formula] for the sake of it.

What kinds of learning strategy have you found effective in helping you deal with your dyslexia?

I have only just come to realise that it is not really about learning work and being good at the work. It's all on technique. These students brought out a book on how to get a first degree and that applies to all degrees. It is all about technique.

Do you use any form of technology and do you find it useful?

It is an electronics course and [there are] not that many demands on the reading and writing.

Do you think that knowing you are dyslexic affects the way you deal with your dyslexia?

It explains why I'm different. I did feel like the 'ugly duckling' at one stage in my life, then [I thought], ' Yes, that's all right because now I'm a swan'.

How about your comprehension?

I'm not sure about the proper psychology of it but it is something like a learning curve. It takes me ages to get the basics but then I can work the hard bits out myself. But for normal people, they fly though the basics and struggle on the hard bits, whereas I'm different. If I can get the basics, then the rest just follows naturally.

How do you think your particular personality influences the way you deal with your dyslexia?

I get dead frustrated. I am a bubbly kind of person anyway. Frustration, that's the main thing really.

Does this frustration affect your self-esteem?

Yes, definitely. I get down in the dumps. Definitely. But what I've taken to doing now is shut them up. You get your normal people and when you're struggling they're flying ahead, going, 'Come on man it's easy, right', so I'll take a particular bit about the basics that I'm struggling with, and the thing is not to sit there and get frustrated. You've just got to bring them down, so they don't understand it either.

Do you tell other students that you're dyslexic?

I don't avoid telling them, but I don't make a point of it either. I don't really.

Is there a stigma attached to being dyslexic?

Oh no. It's dead cool these days. People pretend that they are. I'll go to parties and meet people who say that they're dyslexic when they're not really. It is a cool thing to be these days. It's [like] when being gay was cool a couple of years ago. I always respected autistic people. I always thought autistic people were geniuses, they were great.

So you have a very positive attitude towards your dyslexia then?

Oh yes, definitely.

What kind of reception do you get when you tell them [other people]?

As I said, nowadays it's OK but in the old days it was 'Oh I'm dyslexic' and people would say 'Oh I'm so sorry'. Nowadays, everyone is [dyslexic]. It's no big deal anymore.

Do you ever ask students or staff for specific help?

Yes, definitely. I always think that the way I put it is the best way and I always want 100%. It's very difficult in English to get 100% but in maths and electronics it's not too difficult. There is only one answer. I get frustrated with lecturers who give me early 90's and I say, 'What have I done wrong here?' and [they] say, 'Nothing wrong'. If there is something wrong with it I want to know why.

Do you ask friends for specific help?

Yes, I do go in and hassle the lecturers with little problems, but very rarely on the course. It's something like a deeper understanding. I [am] definitely a troublemaker, I can see that in their eyes.

Are there any situations that you find particularly difficult or embarrassing because of your dyslexia?

I don't think so. I'm not really bothered about it. At school I used to be. Early on when the special teacher used to come in I used to hate that, I used to have to get up. He would say, 'Where is Henry? He has got his extra English.' It was really bad then. Nowadays I'm almost proud about it.

How about problems in everyday life, like filling forms in?

Forms are a bit horrible. You've just got to say 'I'm dyslexic, you fill it out', and she does [it].

You're fairly confident about asking people to do that then?

Oh yes, no problems at all. In the same way if her transistor radio was broken behind her desk and she is trying to fix it and I came along she might say 'Oh, I'm not an electrician, you fix this'. It's what everyone is good at you know. I don't mind being bad at English.

Have you ever felt isolated at university, or when you were younger, because of your dyslexia?

No, not really. It's because they found out early on.

How about in university life?

I don't think it has. I don't really think that my tutors can tell that I'm dyslexic because there is not much written work and what [there] is [is] word processed, mainly conceptual things.

Do you know or meet up with other dyslexic students at the university?

Sometimes, you get a lot of chip-on-the-shoulder dyslexics and they really irritate me. They've got this really big chip on the shoulder.

They really think that they are special cases. It's like people in wheel-chairs, you get some who go down the pub playing snooker and everything and you get another one in a crowded street shouting 'Get out of my way'. I find that a lot of dyslexic people have got a chip on their shoulder. I don't think that it's a special case at all. It's not a disadvantage at all.

Would it help you to meet other dyslexic students?

I wouldn't mind. It would be good to talk, just to decide. You always get told about dyslexia and I haven't got a clue about it and they [the diagnostic characteristics] just don't add up. I don't get this, that and the other. I often find it's not the case. A lot of my worst complaints about it aren't the ones that are told to you. It would be nice to talk to others. But I'm not sure about dyslexia and its existence. I don't think it really exists to be honest.

Do you think that your dyslexia will have a bearing on the kind of job you do when you leave university?

I would be good at a phone job. I wouldn't do a written communica-tions type of thing, or [something where] you had to research a lot of books and scan reading. It does have an influence. Or I could pick something where it was a benefit. I wouldn't pick something where it was a hindrance.

Do you anticipate that having dyslexia will give you difficulties once you've left university?

Yes. Trouble is, I don't perceive myself as having difficulties.

In general, how do you feel at the moment about being dyslexic?

I constantly weigh up its good and bad points. Most of the time it has been a benefit, about 80% of the time. Five per cent of the time I do think actually I am happy about being dyslexic, especially at revision time, where it takes me so long to revise, and other people just read it off and it goes in. They enter the exam and spurt it all out. They couldn't build the thing they're talking about. They are good at suck-ing it in and spurting it all out again.

Is there anything that I have not raised in the interview that you would like to talk about?

[Silence]

You mentioned earlier your doubts over the existence of dyslexia?

This was first put to me by this child psychologist who deals mainly with autistic children, and she thought that dyslexia was more of a learning difficulty than a specific learning difficulty. I was actually arguing the case for dyslexia saying, 'No, no, no you need structured multisensory input', but afterwards I was thinking about it, like you mentioned earlier where the words move around, and saying, ' Oh they [autistic children] must be dyslexic'. Do you draw the line around learning difficulties and everyone's got a different one, and is there a constant type that can be called dyslexic? Where do you draw the line of what is and what isn't? At the [Dyslexic] Institute there is a lot of young kids and they're very much like me in that they've got these great plans, and you get other ones that haven't done anything at all. The only thing you can say about them is that they can't read or write very well. I don't know whether it is dyslexia or not.

Comment

Henry's interview provides interesting insights into the nature of dyslexia. It is clear that he sees it as more than a problem with decoding words when reading or producing the correct spelling when spelling. For him it is principally a problem of understanding what he reads – of grasping the concepts in the message. Once he understands the basics, for which he is heavily reliant on text, he is confident that he has the intellectual ability to extrapolate, make inferences and understand the more complex ideas. Having to respond under time pressure, being 'put on the spot', is a particular problem, preventing understanding, which frequently comes later. When writing he regards his incorrect spellings as being more a problem of the idiosyncratic spelling system than of his dyslexia, a point he makes very forcefully. On the other hand he does experience problems in structuring his thoughts and expressing them within the conventions of writing.

Compared with some of our other interviewees, Henry has been particularly fortunate in the attitudes of significant others. His parents were clearly very supportive, and one can perhaps conclude, from the fact that he does not mention it, that his childhood peers did not treat him as being in any way different. One suspects that this was a function of his teachers' attitude, which seems generally to have been one of casual acceptance. It's worth contrasting this with the negative attitudes of other dyslexics' school experiences. His current peers even seem to regard his problem as having a certain social cachet. The only negative attitudes seem to have come from his university tutors, who may see him as a 'troublemaker' because of his persistent questioning and insistence on understanding every aspect of a topic.

Henry's own attitude to his dyslexia seems ambivalent. The interview is peppered with contradictions. On the one hand, there is his acknowledgement of the real-world problems his dyslexia creates: reading aloud, filling in forms, comprehending text, having to choose his degree course appropriately, and having to trim or even change his career path. His predominant emotional response to these obstacles has always been one of intense frustration. On the other hand, a number of statements suggest that he minimises or even denies his disability. This inconsistency is surely the consequence of a very human attempt to put his disability into perspective. He has to reconcile the fact there are a number of things he can't do with the fact that he has many talents: good oral communication, good understanding (given time), practicality, intuition, inventive talents, and coming up with ideas. His strategy for dealing with these contradictions is one of constantly weighing up his strengths and weaknesses. The oscillations between frustration and denial probably reflect the relative weight he gives these strengths and weaknesses at any given time. The important point is that, in spite of frustration, over the longer term he seems well able to take account of his weaknesses and play to his strengths.

In conclusion, Henry had adopted a very healthy strategy for coping with his dyslexia. Some of this is undoubtedly due to his generally positive experiences with significant others but most of the credit must go to him for trying to put his disability into perspective.

Chapter 12
Summary and
Conclusions

This chapter attempts to summarise the themes that emerge from the student interviews in Chapters 3 – 11, to highlight the main issues that are raised and to make some suggestions for future ways forward to meet the needs of this group. It is divided into subsections that correspond to the main issues that emerged from the interviews. It is important that the reader should remember the following caveats, which relate to the capacity for generalisation of the points made in this chapter.

Firstly, it must be remembered that the students were responding to an interviewer who is himself dyslexic and who was empathic and encouraging at all times, interpolating small remarks or questions in order to encourage the students to describe fully their experiences. The context of the interview was therefore one in which the students might perceive themselves to be 'at home' with someone whose experience in some ways matched their own. This may have permitted them to speak of experiences in a freer way than with another, less empathic interviewer, but also may have created a bias, involuntarily encouraged by the interviewer, towards aspects of experience and issues that were focal points for the interviewer.

The second point to be remembered is that interviews were not also conducted with the control subjects in our study (see Chapter 2) and therefore we do not have a similar qualitative record of their experiences of school and university. Some of the statements made about the dyslexic students may equally be true of the control subjects; they too may have negative perceptions of their school experiences and have current problems in obtaining meanings from text, in organising their essays, in making adequate notes, in speaking in seminars, in finding their way around the library. More mature students in the control sample may also have greater self-awareness and understanding of their preferred learning styles than the younger members. This overlap between the experiences of 'normal' students and those with specific learning difficulties or dyslexia is, as discussed in the Introduction, endemic to the controversies around 'defining dyslexia'. There is no clear-cut boundary surrounding the 'syndrome' of difficulties – there are degrees of difficulty in many areas of functioning, showing varying degrees of severity from extreme to moderate to mild. Understanding of the nature of these difficulties and their interrelationship in development is still in its infancy. Much research remains to be done to clarify the picture.

Perception of School Experience

It must be recognised that the accounts that our subjects give of their schooldays are their perceptions in retrospect and, as such, are shaped by the multiplicity of factors that shape our recall of the past. In general, the students in our sample could be said to have fairly negative perceptions of their school experience. Some of these perceptions are of punishment and humiliation owing to their teachers' perception of them as being lazy and failing to work hard enough to achieve their potential. Generally, these are the perceptions of the older students in our sample, who attended school at a time when dyslexia was not recognised as a disability for which pupils should be given allowances and with which a school should give the pupil specific help. They have memories of being physically punished and bullied and recall their school experience as a disaster that has left a permanent scar. Others, younger and with perhaps less severe difficulties, explain that their schools, even when informed of the 'diagnosis', were very dismissive of the category and unwilling to make any concessions to the pupil's difficulty. Similar painful perceptions of schooldays by adult dyslexics are related by other authors (Osmond, 1993; Barga, 1996).

Protective factors

Some of our students, however, see their schooldays in a less negative light, and several factors stand out as creating a more positive experience for these students. These can be seen as *protective factors*. One of these factors would appear to be early identification. A student who speaks very positively in the preceding chapters of his school experience is Henry, who was identified early and whose teachers recognised his difficulties. In our larger sample there were also two other students, whose interviews are not included in the previous chapters, who were identified early and whose identification was accepted by their schools. It is possible that this early identification and recognition of the nature of their difficulties enabled these three students to avoid the stigma of being called lazy and stupid, and the consequent confusions and lowering of their self-esteem. Early identification has many benefits in that it not only alerts teachers and parents to the problem and allows appropriate early intervention to take place, but it also alters the child's self-perception and others' perception of the child – perceptions that will be incorporated into the child's self-concept. The pupil's academic self-concept is one dimension of a multi-dimensional concept of self, which has been defined as a construct embodying a person's experiences and evaluations of interactions with people and the environment as well as individual reinforcement patterns and the history of successes and failures in past interactions (Bracken, 1992). Feelings of worth that are incorporated into an individual's self-concept are considered to have a profound effect on a child's developing sense of self (Owens, 1993; Harter, 1990). Self-concept and self-esteem are discussed later in the chapter in the section headed 'Self-esteem'.

Another protective factor that emerges from some of the transcripts is the support that some teachers were able to give. Some teachers were particularly sensitive and receptive to the difficulties of the student and were able to provide appropriate support. For example, Peter talks of teachers who were sensitive to his problems, and Janet talks of teachers who were supportive and helpful towards her. In general, however, it is painful and difficult experiences that stand out most clearly. Often, the students apparently perceived the support which they were offered as being inappropriate – learning to spell baby words, or being placed in a group where 'the rest of the morons did not want to work'. If we try to build a picture of the school life of these students it would be too easy to dismiss their teachers as ignorant and unsympathetic. We must remember that primary education for some of these students took place at least 20 years ago when literacy failure was less well understood. Also, it must be recognised that, among those pupils who were failing to achieve satisfactory levels of literacy, the students in our sample were particularly confusing to deal with, as they were probably of above-average intelligence, and their levels of oral skills much higher than their literacy skills. To many teachers, their appalling written work may have appeared to be the result of a slovenly attitude rather than an inability to spell and produce well-written, well-organised work. Do teachers use humiliation and ridicule as a means to rule their class-rooms and as a method to get the best out of their pupils? For the struggling pupil even one teacher who uses these methods will prob-ably stand out in their mind as a formative experience, though coun-terbalanced by many other teachers who did not use these techniques.

In the past, recognition of the existence of dyslexia has been the centre of an ideological struggle (see Pumfrey and Reason, 1991, Chapters 1 and 2, for an excellent summary). Many teachers were educated at a time when dyslexia was unheard of or considered to be a middle-class excuse for a slow child. Over the last decade and a half, partly as a consequence of pressure from interested groups, partly as a consequence of legislation, a general recognition has been developed of a category of children with specific learning difficulties, including those with dyslexia, who have special educational needs (see Pumfrey and Reason, 1991, for the results of a survey of LEAs). However, the straitened finances of LEAs make providing sufficiently for the needs of such pupils impossible, and research and evaluation of teaching and learning methods in this area is also severely constrained.

Another factor that can be extremely protective towards pupils in difficulties is parental support. Yet the idea of dyslexia as a middle-class syndrome promoted by the over-anxious or interfering parent as an excuse for their lazy or unintelligent children is perhaps evident from the account given by some of the students of the experiences of their parents. A similar graphic account of a parental struggle to have a child's problems recognised and provided for is given by Osmond (1993). Several of the students in our sample mention the very positive support given to them by their parents and speak of their parents' struggle with the school to have the nature of their difficulties recognised. Henry, Jenny, Janet and Caroline (with reser-vations) all received a great deal of support from their parents, who struggled on their behalf. Other students received little help – or their parents believed that the teachers were right and that they should not question their judgement. Important factors in differenti-ating between those parents who provided support and those parents who did not seem to be age and parental educational level. Those who did not receive such support from their parents were either older (30+) and had received their school education when knowl-edge of dyslexia was fairly limited, or their parents were less educated. It does seem that the parents who were supportive can be characterised as having higher levels of education themselves, and therefore higher expectations for their children, and also a greater awareness of the mismatch between the child's reasoning abilities and literacy skills and of the possible explanations for this.

The effects that these perceived school experiences had upon the students are mixed. It appears that there is, for most of the students, a continuing influence of their school experiences on their current university experience. On the one hand, the students perceive themselves as being motivated to 'show them' (the teachers) and to prove themselves as cleverer or more successful than their teachers had predicted. However, several dwell upon the anxiety with which the experience has left them and the effects upon their image of themselves as lacking in worth and less able than others. Some are angry and frustrated, others anxious and lacking in confidence. Janet talks of the scars of school. Andy says 'no matter what I do, it's never good enough'. As discussed in the Introduction, evidence from research in Britain and in the USA into the effects of learning disabilities in school on later adult adjustment suggests that adults in the community show no higher rates of disturbance or anxiety than the normal population. Little, however, is known about the effects of continuing education on the levels of anxiety in this group. There is a pertinent study reported by Barga (1996) of a group of 9 students with a variety of learning disabilities following different degree courses in a college in the USA. The results suggest that when students use negative coping strategies (i.e. strategies which attempt to cover up their problems) then anxiety, stress and tension result.

Perceptions of the Label

It is interesting to speculate about what some, or all, of these students might have done had they not acquired the label 'dyslexic'. The very important formative effects of this 'diagnosis' are evinced again and again in the interview transcripts. Nearly all at some point have been labelled otherwise as stupid or lazy, and some, for example, Janet, Peter and Andy, internalised and lived with this self-image for many years. As Janet says, she feels that perhaps she ought not to be at university, that she is not good enough, that she should be at the bottom of the class. Many of them tell of the great relief that they felt when they were told that they were dyslexic and need no longer consider themselves to be unintelligent. As Patrick says: 'It was like a massive weight had lifted off my shoulders and suddenly I wasn't stupid any more.' If these individuals had not been given this new perception of their difficulties would they have gone forward to take up the challenge of university degree course?

All the students discuss the positive and the negative, private and public effects of the label. Privately, the positive effects are apparently the understanding of their own past experiences in a different light with the consequent improvement of self-image, the development of self-awareness in relation to dealing with the difficulties they have and the motivating power of the challenge of dyslexia. Publicly, the label can also be traded for support of various sorts, such as receiving a disability grant or extra time for examinations, and can be seen as opening doors that might otherwise be closed to someone with an apparently low level of literacy. The negative public effects of the label are the stigma that the students perceive the label to carry in the eyes of at least some others – the automatic categorisation as incompetent. Tutors may be affected and give poorer grades. Employers will not be so keen to have someone who is dyslexic and cannot spell. Others may hold you up to ridicule, either because they do not believe in the condition or because you are an easy butt for simple jokes which play on words. Privately taking on board the concept may also have negative effects on motivation – it can be used as a cop-out, so that challenges are not undertaken. The disability could be seen as an excuse for taking an easier path through life. Barga (1996) also discusses the perceptions and effects of the label among her students. She distinguishes between labelling, stigmatisation and gatekeeping (denial of access to opportunities or conditional access), and suggests that the label, although having positive effects for the students in making sense of their academic experiences and obtaining help, can also act as a barrier to education by creating stigmatisation and gatekeeping by individuals and institutions.

Understanding of Dyslexia

If we were able to trace the development of the understanding of each individual of the nature of their dyslexia this would give us important insights into the condition. Studying the transcripts, we see that the concepts of 'dyslexia' held by all these individual students are quite varied. All were relieved to receive the label in the first place. All seem to see it as something which is 'not their fault' and as something they were born with, which will remain with them for the rest of their lives – something constitutional and genetic. They see themselves as different. Several of the students mention that their brains do not seem to work in quite the same way as other people's, and that they think in different ways from normal people.

On the other hand individual understanding of the meaning of the label can be seen to encompass a varying range of difficulties. Some see it as purely a difficulty with literacy skills, others see it as far more pervasive, affecting the organisation of many aspects of their lives. The concept of the label developed by each individual, according to their accounts, appears to depend on several factors – first, the age at which they first come to understand that they are dyslexic, and that this in some way makes them 'different' from others. Those who have lived with the label for some time, such as Henry, appear to develop a fairly complex concept of the syndrome. He says at first, 'I think that dyslexia is far deeper than just problems with English … It's a learning difficulty. It's not tied to English at all', but then later talks about his doubts about the existence of dyslexia and says, 'Do you draw a line around learning difficulties and everyone's got a different one, and is there a constant type that can be called dyslexic?' Second, the individual concept of dyslexia also apparently depends on the particular problems with which each student is faced. Those with very severe reading and writing problems, such as June, dwell on this aspect of the syndrome to the exclusion of others. Those whose reading and spelling problems, such as Jenny, are not so overt and often talk of other associated difficulties such as short-term memory deficits, which affect many areas of functioning. Caroline dwells on her recently developed understanding that her inability to organise her life, including her studies, is 'dyslexic' and she considers that her dyslexia is just as much of a handicap to her social life as to her academic one. Peter, who is now 42 and has received cognitive therapy to help him to come to terms with his difficulties, at the end of his interview says: 'The dyslexic problem … tends to affect your whole life … it affects relationships and forming relationships … you have to develop those skills perhaps ten years later … it often might ruin someone's entire life.' It can be seen from this summary that the concepts of dyslexia and the nature of its effects have developed and changed with time as these people are faced with new experiences and with new challenges in living and learning.

As has been described in Chapter 1, there is continuing controversy surrounding the nature and existence of dyslexia. It seems, from our sample, that the range of difficulties, their patterns of development and degrees of severity vary enormously between individuals. A higher level of intellectual functioning is apparently a protective factor that all our students share in that they are able to value at least some of their own abilities at school – most of them are able to cite some instances or generalisation of their ability to cope with information and knowledge when not presented in written form. The processes involved in learning to read are evidently separate from general reasoning processes, as is shown by the students in our sample. It is apparent that further research in higher education is required to ascertain the types of support that would benefit individuals with a variety of learning difficulties in this challenging context.

Current Difficulties

There is a fairly limited amount of research into the academic difficulties of dyslexic students, which is discussed in the section in Chapter 1 entitled 'Research on Literacy Difficulties'. The academic difficulties our sample currently experience and describe are, however, very varied and range from severe disabilities in reading and writing for some students, who require the use of a reader and an amanuensis during timed work, to residual spelling problems for some students, whose main difficulties lie in comprehending and constructing organised text. Most of our sample could, however, generally be characterised as having mild to moderate literacy problems. The most commonly reported difficulties are with spelling, particularly the spelling of the shorter common words. Many of the students also report comprehension problems, difficulties in organising their writing, in note-taking, and difficulties with short-term memory and general organisation. Even though many of them have overcome their reading difficulties, there remain many problems that could be attributed (as Henry says) to a learning difficulty, which is particularly evident in the acquisition of literacy because of the nature of the processing required, but which may affect many other aspects of development. Caroline is an example of a student who sees her dyslexia as being principally evident in her difficulties in organising many aspects of her life. Interestingly, writers such as Thomson and Watkins (1990) suggest that the majority of children with dyslexia are characterised by general organisational difficulties in addition to their difficulties in acquiring literacy.

If we take a closer look at the major difficulties the students encounter it is possible to identify, firstly, the specific nature of these difficulties and, secondly, the strategies the students use to assist in dealing with the resulting problems in coping with their university degree studies.

Reading

Most of the students mention that reading remains a problem in that the time they need to comprehend a text is much greater than that required by their peers. They comment that although they may read through a passage once they cannot take in its meaning and have to read and re-read the text in order to relate the surface decoding of the words to a meaningful representation of the text. Andy says that his reading is very slow. He jumps ahead and skips lines, and then realises that he is reading a line he has already read 'and that produces a sense of absolute rage and frustration'. He often asks his girlfriend to read to him. Similar problems in maintaining their place in reading are reported by Jenny and Sean. Jenny states, 'It's a problem getting from one line to the next'; and Sean says, 'I jump between lines. I'll come to an end of a line and I'll be two lines down and between those I'll start moving up and down the lines', and adds, 'some passages I cannot comprehend at all'. This anecdotal description of the reading experience seems to suggest that part of the problems for dyslexics may stem from a difficulty in controlling eye movements. Stein (1991) puts forward cogent arguments for the case that visuospatial impairments cause reading difficulties. However, much recent experimental evidence supports the hypothesis that such difficulties in eye movement, although common in dyslexics (Stanley, Smith and Howell, 1983), are related to problems in linguistic processing of the text and that the problems lie with the verbal mediation process rather than with general perceptual processing (Pumfrey and Reason, 1991). The problems that the students experience in associating meaning with the text create the difficulty in eye-movement control. Their developmental difficulties in acquiring reading skills are the source of the development of inappropriate eye movements in relation to text rather than the reverse. It must be said that the jury is still out on this controversy and further research evidence is needed to resolve the issue.

The only student who mentions a strategy to deal with this problem is Andy, who says, 'With closely written stuff I like to put a card beneath to block out the words underneath so that my eyes aren't strained and I'll point.' Jenny and Sean do not mention any methods they have used to overcome similar difficulties.

Not all students report visual difficulties. Students such as Caroline, Janet and June do not report the difficulties in keeping their place in the text, but do report difficulties in taking in meaning. Janet says, 'I find comprehension hard and I really need to read it twice to actually grasp it.' Caroline says that, although her speed of reading is similar to her friends', she read sentences but does not take them in. June says, 'It takes me a long, long time to read and re-read before it can connect. I seem to have to take a hundred times longer if I don't understand sometimes to try and read and find out, to get it connected'; she feels that 'many people in the class connect these things straight away'.

Several strategies to overcome this difficulty are mentioned by students. Taking longer over reading texts in order to assimilate the meaning is mentioned by all. Jenny also says: 'If I want to read and take anything in it takes a long time and I have to sort of stop and highlight something or underline it really.' The necessity to obtain photocopies of texts for this purpose is obvious and is a strain on the budget of under-funded students. As Andy says, 'I spend a fortune on photocopying things and enlarging things ... photocopying things is not an added bonus for dyslexic students. It's a must'. Some students, such as Andy, ask someone else to read the text to them and also have been able to have a reader during examinations. Others, such as Sean, do not attempt to cope with all the reading, but skim through texts to gain an outline of the main ideas, developing their understanding through discussion.

Difficulties in accessing text also lead to difficulties in organising and retaining the information contained within it. Some of the students mention very clear and definite strategies that they have used. Andy, one of the most disabled of the sample, is studying for a degree in the vast and wordy subject of law. He describes how he has narrowed down the amount of reading he has to do by working out the examination structure and concentrating on only the necessary number of topics. He then uses the Buzan memorisation techniques, using visual imagery and associations. He also uses mnemonics such as beating a rhythm and a method of hierarchically structuring information taken from one of his leisure interests, horse-racing. Other students, such as Sean, mention their difficulties in remembering necessary information (derivations in his case), but have not evolved specific strategies to help with the problem. Sean's key strategy for learning is talking about a subject, which enables him to formulate and remember information. He says, 'If I banter work backwards and forwards with someone I can learn a hell of a lot. Getting rid of books completely and talking with someone.'

Spelling

As with reading, all our students report some problems with spelling correctly, particularly with commonly occurring words. As Jenny says, 'When I'm writing an essay I'll spell one word differently the whole way through the essay. I just spell it how I say it.' Patrick relates that comments come back from tutors such as 'good attempt spoilt by bad spelling'. He finds that 'there are red marks on all the spelling mistakes' and it is always 'good effort, shame about the spelling'. Caroline says that she has difficulty with words like 'weather, hoping, hopping. I'm not convinced when they've got two Ps in them, or Cs, or advise and advice. I'm not very good at distinguishing subtle differences between letters. I find, because I teach children, they'll ask me for something really simple like how do you spell "brown" and I get it completely wrong and I find the second I start panicking about it I can't spell anything.'

The principal strategy reported for dealing with this difficulty is to use a word processor with a spellchecker, but many report difficulties in using this, as, when presented with a list of possible words, they are unsure as to which one is correct. Other students use proofreading or peer-checking of their work to correct their mistakes. Some students also acknowledge that they select simple, familiar words in order to avoid spelling problems. On the other hand, Henry, who is very positively assertive about dyslexia, copes by deriding our spelling system and says, 'I don't put an importance on spelling like everyone else does ... Really a lot of it is redundant.' As discussed in Chapter 1, this difficulty with spelling may generally lead tutors to have a poorer impression of their work than otherwise would be the case.

Writing

A number of the students discuss their difficulties in producing satisfactory written work. A range of difficulties are mentioned apart from spelling. Caroline discusses her difficulties in organising her ideas into paragraphs: 'I put paragraphs in and I move them about, then I forget which bit is to go into which paragraph or I start writing a paragraph which is totally irrelevant to somewhere else.' June discusses the fact that even punctuation is a problem to her. Sean says that his essays do not make sense because the commas and full stops and other punctuation marks are in the wrong place. Janet talks about the limitations of her vocabulary and her need to develop a strategy to use a wider variety of words. 'Some of the things my friends write, they write it in these posh fancy, big, long words and it sounds so much better than my work.' Patrick discusses his difficulty in structuring words together to explain something. He can write facts, one after another, but has great difficulties turning something into a paragraph, an explanation or a report. He finds it difficult to make the connection between points and to introduce things at the right time. June says 'without a computer I am lost ... I write as if I'm speaking it and of course that's not proper English or grammar and I don't see my mistakes.'

Producing satisfactory written work is one of the primary demands of many academic university courses. A variety of strategies to assist with this problem are employed by the students. Again, taking a long time to structure and think through and logically organise the content of an essay is mentioned. Using a computer with a word processor is seen as an absolute godsend by many of the students. This is must succinctly described by June, who says, 'I have to get the information on the computer. If it doesn't ring true then I know I've got gaps missing and I find the gaps and put it in. Thank God for the computer because I can jiggle it all around until I think the structure looks right.' The other principal resource for these students appears to the assistance that others are willing to give. Thus Janet will show a plan to her tutor before she starts to write. Caroline and Janet will ask friends or others on the course to read and comment on their work. Andy has received help from the university support services. Others such as Henry have deliberately chosen courses that do not require much writing. Many of the students, when asked what help should be offered to dyslexic students, say that they would find it particularly helpful to have help with essay-writing.

Handwriting and note-taking

Handwriting is another bugbear. Andy, for example, describes his handwriting as looking like something that has crawled across a page. Word-processing assignments has therefore proved an invaluable tool for these students. Without this aid it is very doubtful whether many of them would cope with their workload. However, word-processing does not help with note-taking, and difficulties with this are frequently reported. There is a difficulty with taking notes at the speed required and also with producing legible notes that can be read back afterwards. Some students, such as June, use a tape recorder, which then requires the laborious process of transcription afterwards. Sean reports that he finds transcription impossible. Other students have friends who allow them to copy their notes or receive some help from their tutors in obtaining photocopies of notes and overheads.

Speaking

An additional difficulty in academic life for some, but not all
students, is oral presentation and discussion of ideas in a structured
form in seminars or group discussion. When presenting in a seminar
many of the students resort to speaking without notes, as reading
aloud from a text or from notes is a problem. Several of them, particularly the women, report a lack of confidence in their ability to
express themselves. Janet says, 'I'm frightened that everybody knows
the answer and I don't. I'm still a bit frightened I'll get called stupid.'
Jenny is afraid of stumbling over words: 'I don't like having to speak
out like that because I think it's going to come out completely wrong
so that puts me off saying things.' Caroline says she is 'all right' at
talking but, on the other hand, she will explain something in a
lecture and people will look and think 'Hmmm!'. She finds that 5
minutes later someone will explain exactly what she meant and the
her lecturer will say 'That's brilliant, that's exactly what we're looking for', and she will think, 'That's just what I've said.' She has difficulty in expressing her ideas logically and, like one or two others, has
difficulty in using notes to help, as this requires referring back to
them, keeping your place, reading etc. On the other hand, some
students report oral presentation as a strength. 'I actually get better
marks because I cannot read off a bit of paper' Sean claims, and
Henry says: 'I'm good at talking. That compensates for my lack of
reading and writing work.' Peter says he has no problem. He loves to
be the centre of attention. He does not use notes and 'it comes over
very natural and relaxed and interesting'. June says that she excels in
discussion. She is one of the best: 'I can express myself and I'm confident and not frightened to speak in public.'

Interestingly, in relation to this point, from the transcripts of these
interviews, it appears that some of the students do have difficulties in
presenting their ideas clearly when speaking. Their thoughts at times
seem to lack connection, topics fall into the conversation without
introduction, and the listener or reader has to work hard to piece
together their meaning. Children with oral language-learning difficulties often have these pragmatic problems. Some of the problems
of our students could be seen as part of a general learning difficulty
that particularly affects language. Dyslexia has been called a 'hidden
speech and language disorder' (Stackhouse and Wells, 1991). Recent
research such as that of Scarborough (1992) on the children of
dyslexic mothers indicates that those children in this at-risk group
who have later reading difficulties are likely to exhibit early difficul-

ties or delays in developing oral-language skills. Snowling (1987) reports that dyslexic children often have a history of late or troublesome speech and language development. Reilly (1991) states that 'it is broadly agreed that the dyslexic child has difficulty organising oral language output as well as reading, writing and spelling'. Further research again is required to elucidate these relationships.

Strategies mentioned by the students as assisting them with this difficulty are prior rehearsal and memorisation of presentations, the use of very simple card cues and the presence of supportive friends.

Other difficulties

Two of the students mention the difficulties they have in finding their way around the library and in understanding and using the cataloguing and reference systems. Their difficulties are obviously not understood by members of the library staff, as the students speak of the rather unsympathetic response they have received from staff when they have requested help. These difficulties can be seen as part of their difficulties with alphanumeric systems and possibly also visuospatial difficulties in translating information from a library map. Andy considers that in this respect it would be better to be blind with a guide dog or a white stick, as at least his difficulty would be obvious and comprehensible.

The effects of dyslexia are, of course, not limited to these students' academic work. The underlying difficulty that affects the acquisition of literacy skills also affects performance in other arenas. Several of the students mention difficulties with short-term memory – remembering telephone numbers, lists, formulas, people's names. Telling right from left is mentioned as another difficulty, as is reading platform numbers and train times, and understanding and using timetables. Organisation of daily schedules is another problem that recurs: keeping appointments, remembering deadlines are seen as major hazards. The problems with literacy also, of course, affect functioning in everyday life – reading signposts, writing notes to friends or to people at work, writing numbers on cheques. Some of them try to avoid situations in which they are required to carry out such tasks in public, recalling occasions in the past of humiliation and embarrassment. Others find strategies to deal with them such as using switch cards, word-processing letters to friends, avoiding leaving notes, relying on close friends to assist with timetables and other minor problems.

It is clear that the students in our sample have adopted a number of strategies to enable them to cope, some of them very positive and constructive, others, such as avoidance of the problems, seemingly rather negative and unhelpful in developing self-confidence, study skills or knowledge of a subject. Barga (1996) divides the strategies used by students in her study into positive 'coping techniques' – behaviours or initiatives the student takes to assist in managing his or her disability – and negative 'passing techniques' – particular behaviours a student engages in that help hide or pass off the disability. As noted above, Barga suggest that when students use negative coping strategies then anxiety, stress and tension result.

As can be seen our students use a mixture of positive and negative coping strategies. Some have a very constructive approach, recognising and facing up to their difficulties, being willing to inform their tutors and peers of their difficulties and searching for methods to improve their skills and to manage their difficulties. Others are less constructive, they have found it difficult to inform others of their problems, and tend to use negative techniques such as avoidance of situations that would show up their problems and the use of easy ways out, for example, using simpler words in essays, not speaking out in seminars, copying out sections of text, missing lectures to avoid having to take notes.

Why do some students have a more constructive approach? It is likely that an important factor in creating this approach is the development of self-awareness and self-understanding. This development itself is no doubt influenced by the interaction of a variety of emotional, personality and environmental factors, which serve to constrain or facilitate a positive approach to controlling the course of life. Aune (1991) points out that a student's understanding and acceptance of his or her strengths and weaknesses and learning disability are essential for achieving a smooth transition from school to college. As noted in Chapter 1, McLoughlin, Fitzgibbon and Young (1994) argue that self-awareness in terms of an understanding of one's strengths and weaknesses is essential to the development of effective compensatory strategies. The gradual development of self-awareness and the many setbacks they encounter are discussed by some of the students. The reframing of experience, which Gerber, Ginsberg and Reiff (1992) suggest is a key to success for learning-disabled adults, is revealed in several of these accounts. This reframing is achieved in a variety of ways, as in the extreme case, through Peter's cognitive therapy, or through the light of June's understanding of her children's development, or just through the new certainty following diagnosis that 'I'm not stupid.'

Because they are faced with a major challenge in gaining access to learning, as part of their developing self-awareness, some at least of our students have become very aware of the learning style that suits them best. There are striking differences between students in this respect. Andy and Sean perhaps provide the biggest contrast – Andy is a person who tends to like to work alone and who systematically analyses and organises his learning, whereas Sean loves to talk and be the centre of attention, and finds his best learning is done in discussion. June is somewhat of a contrast. Despite the fact that she excels in class discussion she does not see this as her main route to learning. She has to work alone with her word processor to organise her thoughts, as she cannot write and listen at the same time. She cannot make the connections straight away, but needs time to assimilate ideas on her own. Janet also says that she is very systematic and methodical in her learning, liking to carefully note down and arrange points to her satisfaction. She is not confident in discussion but finds that friends are very supportive and helpful in looking at her work, and suggests that the type of support she would like would be a critical discussion group focusing on written work. These students seem to be very aware of their preferred learning styles and to have devised patterns of working which suit them.

Other students in our sample are more confused and appear less aware of ways of using their own strengths and coping with their weaknesses. Patrick is very anxious and is getting behind with his work. He says, 'I lie awake at night and everything is flowing through my mind, things that I have done, things that I should have done, what I should be doing, the work that I have missed and the little work I have done.' Or, as Jenny says: 'I've never really wanted to say anything to teachers. I've not really liked going up and making excuses. No, I'd rather suffer in silence than go and say anything.' On the whole, it is the older members of our sample who have developed greater self-awareness and clearer strategies. The younger members of the sample, Caroline, Patrick and Jenny, are less clear about their preferred learning styles. It is quite likely that this pattern is reflected in the general student population. Mature students may well tend to be clearer in their understanding of their strengths and abilities and to understand how best to organise their learning. Richardson (1994,1995) reviews the literature in this area and suggests that this is indeed the case.

The differences in the preferred learning styles and abilities of the students are of great interest and suggest the need further research to develop our understanding of the relationship between different types of ability and types of learning. Gardner (1987) has suggested that there are seven types of intelligence and these he translates into seven different styles of learning. It is interesting to use his framework to look at our students' subject choices at degree level; to a large extent, these choices shape the type of learning that will be required of the students. All these students have problems with one style of learning – linguistic. Some students have either demonstrated a special ability or intelligence for another type of learning or, as in the case of Henry, deliberately chosen a path that does not involve much linguistic learning. These students are using what Gardner terms either spatial intelligence (as in the fine arts) or logical/mathematical intelligence (as in science or maths) and have developed their talents and abilities correspondingly. There is no statistical information about the rates of dyslexia in different higher education courses, however, anecdotally, dyslexia is said to be common among both engineering students and those in the visual arts. One of Jenny's friends, who is an engineering student, says: 'You know there are so many dyslexic people doing engineering and I hate getting in a group with them because they can't write.' Robinson and Blair (1995) find that the writing skills of engineering students are generally low in standard and suggest that special training is required if the students are to meet professional requirements. Information from a student on a visual arts course indicated that there is a high rate of dyslexia expected on the course, as there is a tickbox for dyslexics to complete on their written assignment top cover sheet.

The paradox here, however, is that 6 of our sample of 16 have chosen educational paths that require linguistic learning – law, education and social sciences. They have not considered their dyslexia as an impediment and have followed their interest or the demands of a chosen career. When questioned as to their choice of degree course most students did not consider their needs as a dyslexic person in making their choice. The paradoxical six, according to Gardner's framework, should not be able to cope with studying their subjects. According to Gardner, those with good linguistic intelligence are good at memorising names, places and dates, and learn best through saying, hearing and seeing words. Access to learning through *seeing* words is not easy for this group, and some of them, such as Caroline and Jenny, mention their difficulties in expressing themselves in spoken words. Yet they are able to cope with understanding the concepts involved, and expressing their understanding sufficiently well to be studying and succeeding at degree level, which suggests that the ability to handle verbal concepts is independent of difficulties in processing input and output. These students are able to see patterns, to handle and organise arguments and ideas, despite difficulties with the normal medium of exchange of ideas. Gardner's theory of multiple intelligences has led to an advocacy of the restructuring of school to accommodate modes of learning and inquiry that do not highlight the deficits of one particular group, but which allow all children paths to success (Hearne and Stone, 1995). Certainly, some of our students have chosen this way of restructuring their experience for themselves by their choice of course. Should they be advised to do so? Should 'dyslexic' students be advised to steer clear of 'wordy' subjects? Research as yet has no answer to this question. Rationally, perhaps, the answer to this question is 'Yes'. However, motivation and interest are probably the key to academic success, therefore students with particular interests may succeed in a subject, despite all the barriers in their way. As, currently at least, the recognised principal means of exchange of information and ideas is the written word, it is important that the needs of all those who wish to gain access to that information and those ideas should be met. Equal opportunities should be there for all and barriers should not be placed in the paths of those who wish to opt for certain subjects.

Self-esteem

Other factors that may be involved in improving self-awareness and helping the student to develop positive strategies are likely to be personal and emotional responses shaped by experience. One such factor, which we attempted to measure, as described in the introductory and methodology chapters, was level of self-esteem. The average self-esteem rating for the dyslexic students was significantly lower than the rating for their matched controls. If we look at the transcripts of the interviews and consider what we know of the process of development of self-esteem, it is not difficult to understand how this has come about. Individuals with low self-esteem have a low estimation of their own worth and a concept of themselves as inferior, inadequate and incompetent. This estimation is based in part on their own self-evaluation and in part on perceived appraisals from significant others (Harter, 1990). As we have seen, many of our students perceived that significant others in their lives, such as teachers and parents, rated them as incompetent and unintelligent.

Andy's self-esteem rating is very low. Andy's description of his feelings about this early school experiences are so graphic as to be heart-rending. He swapped his pen from hand to hand and his hand was tied to a chair with a crepe bandage. 'Then there was this sense of fear.' People said to his grandmother within his hearing, 'He's terribly slow. I don't think he's going to do very much.' At the stage of entering junior school he was starting already to feel an absolute failure. He was bullied. He did not know what was going on. He was humiliated in front of the class by having to hold up a piece of work that he felt looked fine. 'So I dragged myself up and again this, feeling of being so small, so stupid. I held up my work, I didn't know what was wrong with it and the whole class gasped.' How does a young person learn to deal with such blows to his self-esteem? Andy's response was to become very withdrawn. He had an interest in all sorts of things but at the back of his mind there was a voice saying 'Forget it – you're not really capable.' As with other students, the label of dyslexic came as an immense relief – he was not stupid. He actually had a sense of purpose for the first time which was wonderful. Andy remains highly critical of his work – 'no matter what I do it's never good enough' – overtones of the past come through loud and clear. He never feels as good as anyone else on the course. He now has to deal with warring messages in his head – perhaps they have made a hell of a mistake letting me on this course, perhaps they have not. The battle has in fact led him to a nervous breakdown and depression owing to a loss of self-confidence. He was coping with bad memories of school, and is still very vulnerable to the criticism of others – an insensitive boss wounded his self-esteem enormously by telling him he was stupid and that he should be neater.

June, whose self-esteem rating is also low, talks about the trauma of school and of punishment and humiliation. She withdrew into herself and by the age of 8 had retreated into a world of her own. She was so ashamed. Her parents accepted the school's judgement that she was unintelligent and did not give her any encouragement.

Patrick, also rated as having low self-esteem, was, like June, quiet and withdrawn when young. He experienced a head teacher who told him that the best thing he could do for him was to buy him a bucket, ladder and sponge so that he can clean windows for the rest of his life – he was beyond redemption. He, too, is a prey to anxiety, sleepless nights, missing lectures, getting behind with his work.

Of the students whose interviews are transcribed here only three had intermediate or high levels of self-esteem. Henry, who was identified early and whose school accepted the diagnosis and whose mother founded an institute for dyslexics, does not describe negative experiences at school. On the contrary, he was 'famous' for being dyslexic. He was told he was not 'thick' he just had a problem that was not of his own making. He talks about frustration and occasional embarrassment – but he is able to attribute these experiences to a factor that is not within his control, something imposed on him rather than of his own creation.

Janet also has an intermediate level of self-esteem, and is very well supported by those around her. Her father recognised her difficulties and supported her when she was at school. She now uses several positive coping techniques, which involve informing others of her difficulties, asking for help and facing up to her difficulties.

The other student with high self-esteem is Peter. He is a very different case from Henry. He is a mature student, aged 42, who also went through hell during his school years, has suffered from mental-health problems, but with the aid of cognitive therapy has been able to reconstruct his image of himself and lay the ghosts of the past.

Of the two other students in the sample of 16 (interviews not reported here) who had average or above-average levels of self-esteem, one who was also identified early (aged 9) had parents who believed in dyslexia. His father was a teacher who was dyslexic himself. His teachers at school also recognised his difficulty and he was not considered to be 'stupid'. The other, who was not assessed until rather later at the age of 13, also had parents and teachers who supported him and believed that he had a problem rather than that he was 'thick'. Neither of these two report unhappy experiences at school.

Considering these cases, we can see that there are very important factors that may act to protect or to destroy self-esteem. The best recipe for protection appears to be early identification of the problem, support from parents, and recognition of the nature of the problem by teachers. For those for whom this protection was not available there is apparently a general lowering of self-esteem, a constant voice in the background telling you that your work is not good enough, you are not good enough, severe self-criticism, possibly leading to depression, insomnia and breakdown. Given this scenario, what ways forward have been shown? It is heartening to find among the students one who suffered difficulties of this nature but yet, as a result of cognitive therapy, has apparently recovered. He has laid those ghosts and is able to put primary school behind him and go forward. Certainly, among the students we talked to were some who felt under pressure and were possibly at risk of depression and anxiety. As such, students may be a special group among poor readers and further study of their mental-health needs is warranted.

Other Protective Factors

Other important protective factors that seem to emerge from the interviews are motivation, other strengths and abilities, and personal assertiveness. A theme that runs through many of the interviews is that of the motivating power of 'the challenge of dyslexia'. The challenge created by the label may be another spur to the development of positive strategies. Here we have a set of individuals who all, to a greater or lesser degree, have struggled to master the necessary skills to give them access to education, the principal medium of education being written language. Owing to their particular difficulties in processing written language, these individuals not only start long after their peers in acquiring the necessary skills, but also suffer problems throughout their lives with accessing information through that medium and of conveying information to others. Why do these individuals not give up the unequal struggle? Why do they persist, many with little support from any quarter, in pursuing a star that may well be forever beyond their reach? Their setbacks have apparently not crushed them into a state of 'learned helplessness'. They remain convinced that they can affect the course of their lives. They believe in themselves. Certainly the acquisition of the label 'dyslexia' has, as we have seen, a very powerful influence. Many of the students testify to the illuminating power of the label. 'Suddenly everything fell into place' – there was a reason for the previous setbacks and humiliations and a new framework for interpreting previous experience; and also a spur to move forward. Most of the students feel that their confidence improved as a result of their assessment. Dyslexics are said to be intelligent people, whose problems are constitutional, not of their own making. All those people in the past who considered them to be lazy and stupid were wrong. Somehow, those voices from the past had to be shown that they were wrong. Sean, for instance, says he was 'knocked to shit' while he was at school and that now he can 'ride anything'. He strikes one as a resilient and determined character whose underlying sense of his own ability enabled him to persist with academic work.

Sean is also a good illustration of an individual who had other strengths that must have had an effect on his developing self-concept. A protective factor for him was probably his very contrasting ability in maths: he was in the top set for maths and in the remedial set for English. To an extent this must have been an important lifeline for him. June also mentions that she excelled at sport: 'No one could compete against me.' Much of her aggression and frustration was expressed through her competitiveness in this area. Other students talk of their good oral ability and how they were able to use that to advantage in class and also socially.

It is interesting also to reflect on the effects that differences in the students' personalities may have had on their personal and emotional responses to their difficulties. Several mention the anger and frustration that they have felt about being dyslexic. Others among their peers have gone forward to achieve status and rewards beyond their grasp. Some of the students in our sample show that they are quite assertive, even aggressive, about their problem. Sean appears to revel in stirring things up; he says of his head of year: 'We hate each other. He really hates me, so now I've got this nice job as class rep and now I'm making his life hell.' His assessment as dyslexic has given him confidence. He tells his boss on work placement that he cannot cope with some written material: 'I just threw it on the carpet and said "I can't do it."' Now he comes across as almost a rather truculent or aggressive person, who apparently does not attempt to appease people. If someone is looking when he is writing a cheque he says he feels like 'poking them in the eye'. Henry also says of himself 'I am definitely a trouble maker', and that he splits hairs and asks awkward questions. Other students however, such as Jenny and Patrick, find it difficult to acknowledge their difficulties and internalise the blame for their problems, becoming anxious and self-critical. Other students, such as Janet, are able to be open about their difficulties and have found support without difficulty. They remain self-critical but can share their negative feelings with others.

University Experience

When asked about their university experiences several of the students are quite positive. Janet says that the support she has received has been 'brilliant', and she has no difficulties in telling her lecturers about her difficulty. Jenny also says that when she finally came round to telling her course leader about her problems, he was very helpful and positive in his response. Caroline has also received a positive and useful response. June found the initial response of the college to her information about her dyslexia was positive, but then the 'college system let her down'. She was promised things that did not appear until the very end of her course. Andy found that, although he 'showed no emotion' in response to the information, his course leader did make arrangements for dictation of his exams and also photocopied and enlarged material for him.

Other students detail some more negative experiences. Peter received everything from indifference to the response that every other student claims they are dyslexic. One tutor had responded that in his view dyslexia was just another one of the menu of excuses that students think up. Sean says that everyone takes it as a bit of a joke – but some are more helpful than others. Henry also describes some difficulties he has had with a tutor who he feels ridiculed his problems.

The students give a variety of responses to the question 'Ideally what sort of support should be available to students?' All consider that it would be helpful to talk to other students with dyslexia in order to share experiences, obtain emotional support and to discuss coping strategies. Others mention the need for help with essay-writing and with spelling and grammar. The use of a word processor is seen as absolutely essential, as are photocopies of relevant material that can be used individually by the students who need a long time to assimilate the material and need to highlight points without having to copy them out. Appropriate support in examination time is mentioned – use of an amanuensis and/or a reader plus extra time to assimilate information or to write. Greater awareness and understanding by staff is considered to be important, help with obtaining good lecture notes, copying materials, advice on essay plans and finding a way through the library system are all mentioned as specific ways in which staff could be helpful to dyslexic students. Some students also mention that specific counselling should be available to counteract the psychological and emotional difficulties that almost inevitably accompany the dyslexic student in an academic career.

Conclusions

The evidence given by these students raises the following concerns and issues, which require attention.

What is dyslexia?

Reading through these interviews of students who all at some time have been given the label 'dyslexic', we have seen very varied patterns of difficulty in acquiring literacy and other skills. It seems very important that further research is carried out into the range and nature of difficulties that could be said to fall within the spectrum of dyslexia or of specific learning difficulties. In order to assist struggling learners and teachers we need to know more of the nature of the underlying difficulties and also of the range of types of teaching and learning strategies that can be developed.

Encouraging academic success in people with dyslexia

Dyslexic students in higher education are an interesting group. Further study of the factors that permit or constrain the academic and vocational development of this group is needed. Our evidence suggests that those who succeed are a determined bunch, not easily deterred from their path, but that some supportive environmental factors may be particularly protective of their mental health and also facilitate their progress.

Primary and secondary education

Environmental factors at this level appear to be early identification of difficulties, parental support, understanding of the nature of their difficulties and suitable teacher support at school. To facilitate the operation of these factors the following recommendations are made:

1. Initial teacher education courses, whether for primary or secondary teachers should all include a substantial element on the identification of specific learning difficulties and on intervention. Teachers should be informed of the social and emotional needs of the child with specific learning difficulties as well as being introduced to current ideas on intervention and learning support.
2. Teachers should be given real support in their attempts to meet the needs of a wide range of students in accessing the National Curriculum. Consistent LEA policies are necessary, which emphasise the importance of early identification and intervention, recognise the needs of dyslexic individuals at school and provide as far as possible for learning support and understanding of the problem throughout the pupil's school career. Many LEAs do try to provide the relevant support, staffing resources and training, but are very constrained by their own budgetary limitations. There is no substitute for the adequate resourcing of special needs support. However, one very important function that LEAs might serve that would be proactive and less expensive is the whole-hearted backing of provision of in-service staff training for all in order that, at the very least, staff awareness of the problem is consistent and some of the psychological damage to individuals might be avoided. It may be that only one teacher ridicules or labels a dyslexic child as stupid, but this can leave a scar that may be difficult for other, more understanding, teachers to remove.

3. There should be consistency among LEAs in the provision of support for students in higher education. At the moment the amount of support received varies from one area to another. Students who need such support should not have to battle for it or be short-changed in their struggle to overcome their disability.

What can be done to help students with specific learning difficulties in higher education?

It is clear that although some lecturers and teachers in higher education are supportive and understanding towards students with dyslexia/specific learning difficulties others are less than sympathetic and helpful. This is understandable as many, possibly the majority of university teaching staff, have received no formal training as educationalists and may have developed their understanding of the learning difficulties of students in a very haphazard fashion. Additionally, until the recent growth of the higher education sector, numbers of students with such difficulties attempting degree courses were few, therefore there has been little need for such understanding. There is, as yet, little systematic published research into dyslexia in higher education although in the last 3 years some institutions, funded by the Higher Education Funding Council, have been investigating the needs of this group. The results of this research has not yet been widely disseminated. However, on the basis of our study and some of the relevant US research, the following points seem clear.

Higher education institutions should adopt mandatory policies in relation to students with specific learning difficulties/dyslexia concerning the following issues:

1. Staff training. Staff should be given training which demonstrates the reality of dyslexia, the nature and diversity of the problems that students will encounter and the role they must take in assisting these students in accessing their particular subject. This training should include an element which raises staff awareness of prejudice and stigma in relation to dyslexia and of the effects of the label on the perceptions and behaviours of others and also of its effects on the self-perception and understanding of the student. The socio-emotional adjustment of individuals with learning difficulties should also be discussed. Staff should be informed of the range of help that may be needed by the student, including photocopying and enlarging, taping of lectures, assistance with essay-writing and note-taking, a reader or an amanuensis.

2. All universities should institute policies that enable students to make their difficulties known on entry to the institution and ensure that from then on the student is aware of the specific services which are available to help.

3. Universities should provide three types of support service for students with learning difficulties:

i. a learning support service to assist the student in developing literacy skills and/or numeracy skills and also to develop learning and coping strategies that will facilitate effective study.

ii. a counselling support service, informed of the developmental difficulties facing dyslexic students, which will, if necessary, provide individual opportunities for students to discuss emotional and social issues, assist them in reframing their problems and in adopting self-help strategies and provide opportunities for the organisation of support groups in which dyslexic students will have opportunities to meet others with similar difficulties and to share their problems, coping strategies and solutions.

iii. a financial advice service, increasingly necessary for all students in these days of ever-diminishing support, which will give appropriate advice to students on the Student Disability Allowance to enable the purchase of a word processor (considered essential by all our interviewees) and the receipt of allowances to pay for necessary photocopying and other resources such as a reader or an amanuensis.

4. Examination policies. All higher education institutions should have coherent policies that are mandatory for all faculties and departments. These policies should ensure that provision is made to cover the range of needs of dyslexic students in examinations from agreed extra time to an amanuensis or word processor as the student's level of disability dictates.

Directions for further research

Finally, there are many areas where further research is needed in order to clarify our understanding of the needs of dyslexic students and students with other specific learning difficulties. The following issues should be addressed.

1. Assessment of individual need. We need to develop some understanding of how this can be done effectively in order to provide appropriate support in studying and during assessments such as examinations.

2. The evaluation of the efficacy of different types of support: learn-

ing, emotional and financial. Each of these issues should be addressed systematically so that the most appropriate solutions can be found to the individual student's problems and time and money are spent effectively.

3. The evaluation of individual coping strategies. This should give us valuable insight into effective coping and enable useful information to be given to students starting out on a university career.

4. The evaluation and development of software/hardware. The ever-increasing flexibility and power of the computer as a tool for learning should facilitate the access of students with literacy difficulties to all types of information and may also be used in itself to develop literacy and numeracy skills. Again, evaluation of the efficacy of the use of different types of hardware and software is essential to inform students and lecturers alike.

5. In order to support and provide for the needs of dyslexic individuals and also to develop our understanding of cognitive and socio-emotional development generally research is urgently needed into the lifetime course of the emotional and social development of dyslexic individuals, and the relationship between this and cognitive aspects of individual development.

Appendix

The purpose of this questionnaire is to help us build an academic and professional profile of respondents. There are five sections:

1. Biographical information
2. At school
3. Between school and university (this is only for those who had time out, for what ever reason, between school and university).
4. At university
5. Future career

Some questions require only a yes or a no. Others require you to circle the appropriate answer. Others are open-ended and require a concise but full answer. If the question doesn't apply to you write n/a.

ALL INFORMATION WILL BE TREATED CONFIDENTIALLY

Biographical Information

NAME:

DATE OF BIRTH:

SEX (male/female):

NATIONALITY:

ETHNIC GROUP:

Caucasian	Afro-Caribbean	Indian subcontinent	Oriental	Other

FIRST LANGUAGE:

COURSE:

YEAR OF COURSE:

FATHER'S OCCUPATION:

MOTHER'S OCCUPATION:

OWN PROFESSION (if appropriate):

ALL EDUCATIONAL INSTITUTIONS ATTENDED
(please list, with dates, stating whether part or full time):

1. _____

2. _____

3. _____

4. _____

5. _____

6. _____

At School

In this section we are interested with your thoughts and opinions when you were at school. Try and remember how you felt then.

1. In general, how did you think you compared, academically, with your classmates?

Primary school:

much worse	worse	average	better	much better

Secondary school:

much worse	worse	average	better	much better

2. In general, were you more anxious or less anxious about school-work than your classmates?

much more anxious	more anxious	about the same	less anxious	much less anxious

3. In general, how did you think your written work compared with your true ability?

Primary school:

much worse	worse	about same	better	much better

Secondary school:

much worse	worse	about same	better	much better

4. Which subject did you like most? Which did you like least?

Primary school: most: least:
Secondary school: most: least:

5. At which subject were you best? At which were you worst?

Primary school: best: worst:
Secondary school: best: worst:

6. Did you take any GCSEs or 'O' levels? If yes, which ones?

Which did you pass? Please give grades.

How did you do compared with your classmates?

much worse	worse	average	better	much better

How did you do compared with how *you* expected to do?

much worse	worse	average	better	much better

How did you do compared with how *your teachers* expected you to do?

much worse	worse	average	better	much better

How did you do compared with how *your parents* expected you to do?

much worse	worse	average	better	much better

7. Did you take any 'A' levels? If yes which ones?

Which did you pass? Please give grades.

How did you do compared with your classmates?

much worse	worse	average	better	much better

How did you do compared with how *you* expected to do?

much worse	worse	average	better	much better

How did you do compared with how *your teachers* expected you to do?

much worse	worse	average	better	much better

How did you do compared with how *your parents* expected you to do?

much worse	worse	average	better	much better

8. **Did you have any specific disability or problem (diagnosed or not) which you think affected your school performance? If yes, what?**

Primary school

Secondary school

9. **Were you given any special help with this problem? If yes, what?**

Primary school

Secondary school

Between School and University

If you came to university directly from school go directly to page 10 otherwise continue

Again, try and answer these questions, when appropriate, on the basis of how you felt and thought at the time.

1. **How old were you when you left school?**
    Why did you leave when you did?
    How old were you when you came to university?

2. **What were you doing, work-wise, in the intervening years? Please list jobs.**
    What was the longest time spent in any one job? Which one?
    Were you ever promoted to a position/positions of responsibility? If yes, to what?
    Did you spend any time unemployed? If yes, about how long *in total*?

3. **Did you have any specific disability or problem (diagnosed or not) which you think affected your work performance and promotion prospects? If yes, what?**

4. **Did you take any GCSEs or 'O' levels in these intervening years?**

If yes, which ones?

At which college(s)?

Which did you pass? Please give grades.

How did you do compared with your classmates?

much worse	worse	average	better	much better

How did you do compared with how *you* expected to do?

much worse	worse	average	better	much better

How did you do compared with how *your teachers* expected you to do?

| much worse | worse | average | better | much better |

How did you do compared with how *your parents* expected you to do?

| much worse | worse | average | better | much better |

5.   **Did you take any 'A' levels in these intervening years?**

If yes, which ones?

At which colleges/institutions?

Which did you pass? Please give grades.

How did your do compared with your classmates?

| much worse | worse | average | better | much better |

How did you do compared with how *you* expected to do?

| much worse | worse | average | better | much better |

How did you do compared with how *your teachers* expected you to do?

| much worse | worse | average | better | much better |

How did you do compared with how *your parents* expected you to do?

| much worse | worse | average | better | much better |

6.   **Did you take any other academic or work oriented courses or qualifications in these intervening years?**

If yes, which ones?

At which colleges/institutions?

Which did you pass?

7. **Generally, when doing these various 'O' levels, etc., how did you think your written work compared with your true ability?**

much worse	worse	about same	better	much better

8. **Did you have any specific disability or problem (diagnosed or not) which you think affected you academic performance?**

9. **Were you given any special help with this problem? If yes, what?**

At University

1. **Which universities or polytechnics did you apply to?**

2. **Why did you choose the universities or polytechnics you applied to?**

3. **Why did you choose the course(s) you did?**

4. **Why did you come to Northumbria?**

5. **Generally, how do you think you compare, academically, with your course peers?**

much worse	worse	average	better	much better

6. **Generally, are you more anxious about academic work than your course peers?**

much more anxious	more anxious	about the same	less anxious	much less anxious

7. **Generally, how do you think your written work compares with your true ability?**

much worse	worse	about same	better	much better

8. **Which aspect(s) of your course do you like most?**

    Which aspect(s) do you like least?

9. **Which aspect(s) of your course are you best at?**

    Which aspect(s) are you worst at?

10. **Do you have any specific disability or problem (diagnosed or not) which you think affects your present academic performance? If yes, what?**

11. **Are you being given any special help or concessions for this problem? If yes, what?**

Future career

1. At school, what *kind* of work or career did you think you would eventually go into?

2. About when (give age if possible) did getting a degree become part of your 'career goal'?

   What influenced the decision to do a degree?

3. What kind of job or career have you in mind now (*be as specific as you can*)?

   What kind of factors have influenced your choice?

4. What may prevent you from doing what you want?

5. Assuming you got into your chosen career, what might prevent you from climbing the ladder as high as you want to go?

THANK YOU FOR YOUR HELP

References

Anderson, K.C., Brown, C.D. and Tallal, P. (1993) Developmental language disorder – evidence for a basic processing deficit. Current Opinion in Neurology & Neurosurgery, 6, 1, 98–106.

Aune, E. (1991) A transition model for post-secondary bound students with learning disabilities. Learning Disabilities Research and Practice, 6, 177–187.

Baker, L. and Lombardi, B. R. (1985) Students' lecture notes and their relation to test performance. Teaching of Psychology, 12, 28–32.

Balow, B. and Bloomquist, M. (1965) Young adults ten to fifteen years after severe reading disability. Elementary School Journal, 66, 44–48.

Barga, N. A. (1996) Students with learning disabilities in education: Managing a disability. Journal of Learning Disabilities, 29, 4, 413–421.

Battle, J. (1992) Culture Free Self-esteem Inventories (2nd edn). Austin, TX: PRO-ED.

Beaton, A., McDougall, S. and Singleton, C. (1997) Editorial: Humpty Dumpty grows up? – Diagnosing dyslexia in adulthood. Journal of Research in Reading, 20, 1 (Feb.)

Bishop, D. V. M. (1989b) Unfixed reference, monocular occlusions and developmental dyslexia – a critique. British Journal of Opthalmology, 73, 81–85.

Brachacki, G.W.Z., Fawcett, A.J. and Nicolson, R.I. (1995) Impaired recognition of traffic signs in adults with dyslexia. Journal of Learning Disabilities, 28, 5, 297.

Bracken, B. A. (1992) Multidimensional Self Concept Scale. Austin, TX. [PRO-ED]

Bradley, L. and Bryant, P. (1985) Rhyme and Reason in Reading and Spelling. Ann Arbour, MI: University of Michigan Press.

Brown, J. I., Bennett, J. M. and Hanna, G. (1981) Nelson-Denny Reading Test Manual (Forms E and F). Boston, MA: Riverside.

Bruck, M. (1985) The adult function of children with specific learning disabilities: a follow up study. In I. Siegal (ed.) Advances in Applied Developmental Psychology. Norwood, NJ: Ablex.

Bruck, M. (1987) The adult outcomes of children with learning disabilities. Annals of Dyslexia, 37, 252–263.

Bruck, M. (1992) Persistence of dyslexics' phonological awareness deficits. Development Psychology, 28, 874–886.

Bryson, M. and Siegal, L. (1986) The development of written language production in normally achieving and learning disabled children. Paper presented at the annual meeting of the Canadian Psychological Association, Toronto.

Cowen, S. E. (1988) Coping strategies of university students with learning disabilities. Journal of Learning Disabilities, 21, 161–164.

Deno, S., Marston, D. and Mirkin, P. (1982) Valid measurement procedures for continuos evaluation of written expression. Exceptional Children, 48, 368–371.

Edgar, E. (1987) Secondary programs in special education: Are many of them justifiable? Exceptional Children, 53, 555–561.

Edwards, J. (1994) The Scars of Dyslexia. London: Cassell.

Einstein, G. O., Morris, J. and Smith, S. (1985) Note-taking, individual differences, and memory for lecture information. Journal of Educational Psychology, 77, 522–532.

Ellis, A. (1993) Reading, Writing and Dyslexia: A Cognitive Analysis. Hove: Lawrence Erlbaum Associates.

Fawcett, A. and Nicolson, R. (1992) Automatisation deficits in balance for dyslexic children. Perceptual and Motor Skills, 75, 507–529.

Fawcett, A. and Nicolson, R. (eds) (1994) Dyslexia in Children. London: Harvester Wheatsheaf.

Fisher, B. L., Allen, R. and Kose, G. (1996) The relationship between anxiety and problem solving skills in children with and without learning disabilities. Journal of Learning Disabilities, 29, 439–446.

Galaburda, A. M., Rosen, G. D. and Sherman, G. F. (1989) The neural origin of developmental dyslexia: Implications for medicine, neurology and cognition. In A. M. Galaburda (ed.) From Reading to Neurons. Cambridge, MA: MIT Press.

Galaburda, A.M., Sherman, G.F, Rosen, G.D.,Abotiz, F. and Geschword, N. (1995) Developmental dyslexia: Four consecutive patients with cortical anomalies. Annals of Neurology, 18,222–223.

Gardner, H. (1984) Frames of mind: The Theory of Multiple Intelligences. London: Heinemann.

Gardner, H. (1993) Multiple intelligences: The theory in practice. New York: Basic Books.

Gentile, L. M. and McMillan, M. M. (1987) Stress and Reading Difficulties: Research Assessment and Intervention. Newark, DE: International Reading Association.

Gerber, P. J., Ginsberg, R. and Reiff, H. B. (1992) Identifying alterable patterns in employment success for highly successful adults with learning disabilities. Journal of Learning Disabilities, 25, 475–487.

Gerber, P. J., Reiff, H. B. and Ginsberg, R. (1996) Reframing the learning disabilities experience. Journal of Learning Disabilities, 29, 98–101.

Gilroy, D. (1993) Dyslexia and Higher Education. Bangor: Dyslexia Unit, University College of Wales.

Goldberg, R. L. (1983) Learning styles, learning abilities and learning problems in college students. Unpublished doctoral dissertation, Clark University, Worchester, MA.

Gottardo, A., Siegal, L. S. and Stanovich K. E. (1997) The assessment of adults with reading disabilities: What can we learn from experimental tasks? Journal of Research in Reading, 20, 1 (Feb.).

Graham, S. (1990) The role of production factors in learning disabled students' compositions. The Journal of Educational Psychology, 80, 781–791.

Greenbaum, B., Graham, S. and Scales, W. (1996) Adults with learning disabilities: Occupational and social status after college. Journal of Learning Disabilities, 29, 167–173.

Hanley, R. (1997) Reading and spelling impairments in undergraduate students with developmental dyslexia. Journal of Research in Reading, 20, 1 (Feb.) 22–30.

Hardy, M. (1968) Clinical follow up study of disabled readers. Unpublished doctoral dissertation, University of Toronto, Canada.

Harter, S. (1990) The determinants and mediational role of global self-worth in children. In Eisenberg, N. (ed.) Contemporary Topics in Developmental Psychology. New York: John Wiley and Sons.

Hartzell, H. and Compton, C. (1984) Learning disabilities: A ten year following. Pediatrics, 74, 1058–1064.

Haslum, M. N. (1989) Predictors of dyslexia? Irish Journal of Psychology, 10, 622–630.

Hearne, D. and Stone, S. (1995) Multiple intelligences and underachievement: Lessons from individuals with learning disabilities. Journal of Learning Disabilities, 28, 7, 439–448.

Hedderly, R. (1996) Assessing pupils with specific learning difficulties for examination special arrangements at GCSE, 'A' level and degree level. Educational Psychology in Practice, 12, 1.

Hill, G. (1984) Learning disabled college students: Assessment of academic aptitude. Unpublished doctoral dissertation, Texas Technical University.

Hughes, C. and Suritsky S. (1994) Note taking skills of university students with and without learning disabilities. Journal of Learning Disabilities, 27, 20–24.

Hulme, C. and Snowling, M. (eds) (1994) Reading Development and Dyslexia. London: Whurr Publishers.

Josselon, R. and Lieblich A. (eds) (1993) The Narrative Study of Lives. Newbury Park, CA: Sage Publications.

Kavale, K. A. and Forness, S. R. (1996) Social skill deficits and learning disabilities: a meta-analysis. Journal of Learning Disabilities, 29, 226–237.

Kiewra, K. A. and Fletcher, H. J. (1984) The relationship between levels of note taking and achievement. Human Learning, 3, 273–280.

Klein, C. (1993) Diagnosing Dyslexia: A Guide to the Assessment of Adults with Specific Learning Difficulties. London: Avanti.

Livingstone, M.S., Rosen, G.D., Drislane, F.W. and Galaburda, A.M. (1991) Physiological and anatomical evidence from a magnocellular deficit in developmental dyslexia. Proceeding of the National Academy of Sciences of the United States of America, 88, 7943–7947.

Lovegrove, W. (1991) Spatial frequency processing in normal and dyslexic readers. In J. Srien (ed.) Visual Dyslexia. Vol. 13 Vision and Visual Dysfunction. London: Macmillan.

Lovegrove, W. (1994) Visual deficits in dyslexia: Evidence and implications. In A. Fawcett and R. Nicolson (eds) Dyslexia in Children. Hemel Hempstead: Harvester Wheatsheaf.

MacArthur, C. and Graham, S. (1987) Learning disabled students composing under three methods of text production: Handwriting, word processing, and dictation. The Journal of Special Education, 21, 22–42.

MacArthur, C., Graham, S. and DeLa Paz, S. (1996) Spellcheckers and students with learning disabilities: Performance comparisons and impact on spelling. The Journal of Special Education, 30, 1, 35–57.

MacArthur, C., Graham, S., Haynes, J. and DeLaPaz, S. (1996) Spelling checkers and students with learning disabilities: performance comparisons and impact on spelling. The Journal of Special Education, 30, 35–37.

Maughan, B. (1994) Behavioural development and reading disability. In C. Hulme and M. Snowling (eds) Reading Development and Dyslexia. London: Whurr.

McGuire, J., Madaus, J., Litt, A. and Ramirez, M. (1996) An investigation of documentation submitted by university students to verify their learning disabilities. Journal of Learning Disabilities, 29, 297–304.

McLoughlin, D., Fitzgibbon, G. and Young, V. (1994) Adult Dyslexia: Assessment Counselling and Training. London: Whurr.

Miles, T. (1993) Dyslexia: The Pattern of Difficulties. Oxford: Blackwell.

Miles, T. and Gilroy, D. (1983) Dyslexia at College. London: Routledge.

Miles, T. R. and Miles, E. (1990) Dyslexia: A Hundred Years On. Milton Keynes: Open University Press.

Moore, L.H., Brown, W.S., Markee, T.E., Theberge, D.C. and Zvi, J.C. (1995) Bimanual coordination in dyslexic adults. Neuropsychologia, 33, 6, 781–793.

Osmond, J. (1993) The Reality of Dyslexia. London: Cassell.

Owens, K. (1993) The World of the Child. New York: Macmillan.

Mosely, D. (1989) How lack of confidence in spelling affects children's written expressionism. Educational Psychology in Practice, 5 (April).

Peer, L. (1994) Dyslexia: The Training and Awareness of Teachers. Reading: British Dyslexia Association.

Phillips, P. (1990) A self advocacy plan for high school students with learning disabilities: A comparative case study analysis of students', teachers', and parents' perceptions of program effects. Journal of Learning Disabilities, 23, 466–471.

Price, L. A., Johnson, J. M. and Evelo, S. (1994) When academic assistance is not enough: Addressing the mental health issues of adolescents and adults with learning disabilities. Journal of Learning Disabilities, 27, 82–90.

Pumfrey, P. and Reason, R. (1991) Specific Learning Difficulties (Dyslexia): Challenges and Responses. London: Routledge.

Rack, J. (1997) Issues in the assessment of adults with reading disabilities: what can we learn from experimental tasks? Journal of Research in Reading, 20, 1 (Feb.) 66–76.

Reilly, J. (1991) The use of tape recorders to develop speaking and listening skills. In M. Snowling and M. E. Thomson (eds) Dyslexia: Integrating Theory and Practice. London: Whurr Publishers.

Richardson, J. E. (1994) Mature students in Higher Education: A literature survey of approaches to studying. Studies in Higher Education, 19, 3, 309–325.

Richardson, J. E. (1995) Mature students in higher education. Studies in Higher Education, 20, 1, 5–17.

Riddick, B. (1995) Dyslexia and development: an interview study. Dyslexia: An International Journal of Research and Practice, 1, 2.

Riddick, B. (1996) Living with Dyslexia: The Social and Emotional Consequences of Specific Learning Difficulties. London: Routledge.

Robinson, C. M. and Blair, G. M. (1995) Writing skills training for engineering students in large classes. Higher Education, 30, 1, 99–114.

Roffman, A., Herzog, J. and Wersham-Gershon, P. (1994) Helping young adults understand their learning disabilities. Journal of Learning Disabilities, 27, 413–419.

Rothstein, L. F. (1993) Legal issues. In S. A. Vogel and P. B. Alderman (eds) Success for College Students with Learning Disabilities. New York: Springer-Veilag

Rudel, R. G. (1985) The definition of dyslexia: language and motor deficits. In F. H. Duffy and F. Geschuimid (eds) Dyslexia: A Neuroscientific Approach to Clinical Evaluation. Boston, MA: Little, Brown.

Runyan, M. K. (1991) The effect of extra time on the reading comprehension scores for university students with and without learning disabilities. Journal of Learning Disabilities, 24, 104–108.

Scarborough, H. S. (1990) Very early language deficits in dyslexic children. Child Development, 61, 6, 1728–1743.

Scott, M. E., Scherman, A. and Phillips, H. (1992) Helping individuals with dyslexia succeed in adulthood: Emerging keys for effective parenting, education and development of positive self-concept. Journal of Instructional Psychology, 19, 197–204.

Shaywitz, S. E. (1996) Dyslexia. Scientific American, November, 98–104.

Singleton, C. H. (ed.) (1997) Dyslexia in Higher Education: Policy, Provision and Practice (Report of the National Working Party on Dyslexia in Higher Education) Hull: University of Hull.

Snowling, M. (1980) The development of grapheme–phoneme correspondences in normal and dyslexic readers. Journal of Experimental Child Psychology, 29, 294–305.

Snowling, M., Nation K., Moxham, P., Gallagher, A. and Frith, U. (1997) Phonological processing skills of dyslexic students in higher education: A preliminary report. Journal of Research in Reading, 20, 1 (Feb.) 31–41.

Speece, D. L. (1987) Information processing sub-types of learning disabled readers. Training Disabilities Research, 2, 2, 91–102.

Speilberger, C.D., Gorsuch, D.L. and Luschene, R.E. (1970) Manual for the State-Trait Anxiety Inventory. Palo Alto, CA: Consulting Psychologists Press.

Spreen, O. (1987) Learning Disabled Children Growing Up: A Follow Up Study into Adulthood. Lisse, Netherlands: Swets and Zeitlinger.

Stackhouse, J. and Wells, B. (1991) Dyslexia: The obvious and hidden speech and language disorder. In M. Snowling and M. E. Thomson (eds) Dyslexia: Integrating Theory and Practice. London: Whurr Publishers.

Stanley, G., Smith, G. A. and Howell, E. A. (1983) Eye movements and sequential tracking in dyslexic and control children. British Journal of Psychology, 74, 181–187.

Stein, J.F. (1991) Vision and language. In M. Snowling and M.E. Thomson (eds) Dyslexia. Integrating Theory and Practice. London: Whurr Publishers

Stein, J. F. (1994) A visual defect in dyslexics? In A. Fawcett and R. Nicolson (eds) Dyslexia in Children. Hemel Hempstead, Harvester Wheatsheaf.

Thomson, M. E. and Watkins, E. J. (1990) Dyslexia: A Teaching Handbook. London: Whurr Publishers.

Vogel, S., Hruby, P. and Alderman, P. (1993) Educational and psychological factors in successful and unsuccessful college students with learning disabilities. Learning Disabilities Research and Practice, 8, 35–43.

Yapp, R. and van der Leij, A. (1994) Automaticity deficits in dyslexia: Evidence and implications. In A. Fawcett and R. Nicolson (eds) Dyslexia in Children. Hemel Hempstead: Harvester Wheatsheaf.

Zigmond, N. and Thorton, H. (1985) Follow-up of post-secondary age learning disabled graduates and dropouts. Learning Disabilties Research, 1, 50–55.

Index